First Steps in Economic Indicators

FT Prentice Hall
FINANCIAL TIMES

In an increasingly competitive world, we believe it's quality
of thinking that will give you the edge – an idea that
opens new doors, a technique that solves a problem, or an
insight that simply makes sense of it all. The more you
know the smarter and faster you can go.

That's why we work with the best minds in business
and finance to bring cutting-edge thinking and best
learning practice to a global market.

Under a range of leading imprints, including
Financial Times Prentice Hall, we create world-class
print publications and electronic products bringing our
readers knowledge, skills and understanding which can be
applied, whether studying or at work.

To find out more about our business publications, or tell us
about the books you'd like to find, you can visit us at
www.business-minds.com

For other Pearson Education publications, visit
www.pearsoned-ema.com

First steps in Economic Indicators

Peter Temple

Prentice Hall
FINANCIAL TIMES

Boston · San Francisco · New York · Toronto · Montreal
London · Munich · Paris · Madrid · Cape Town
Sydney · Tokyo · Singapore · Mexico City

PEARSON EDUCATION LIMITED

Head office:
Edinburgh Gate
Harlow CM20 2JE
Tel: +44 (0)1279 623623
Fax: +44 (0)1279 431059

London Office:
128 Long Acre
London WC2E 9AN
Tel: +44 (0)20 7447 2000
Fax: +44 (0)20 7447 2170
Website: www.business-minds.com

First published in Great Britain in 2003

© Pearson Education Limited 2003

The right of Peter Temple to be identified as Author
of this Work has been asserted by him in accordance
with the Copyright, Designs and Patents Act 1988.

ISBN 0 273 65911 1

British Library Cataloguing in Publication Data
A CIP catalogue record for this book can be obtained from the British Library

This publication is designed to provide accurate and authoritative information in regard to the subject matter covered. It is sold with the understanding that neither the authors nor the publisher is engaged in rendering legal, investing, or any other professional service. If legal advice or other export assistance is required, the service of a competent professional person should be sought.

The publisher and contributors make no representation, express or implied, with regard to the accuracy of the information contained in this book and cannot accept any responsibility or liability for any errors or omissions that it may contain.

10 9 8 7 6 5 4 3 2 1

Typeset by Pantek Arts Ltd, Maidstone, Kent
Printed and bound in China

The Publisher's policy is to use paper manufactured from sustainable forests.

About the author

Peter Temple was born in West Yorkshire and has a degree in economics and statistics from the University of Wales, where he won the Eames Prize for Economics in 1970. He is a former member of the London Stock Exchange and a Fellow of the Securities Institute. He spent the first 18 years of his working life in fund management and investment banking, turning to full-time writing in 1988.

His articles cover a wide variety of topics on business, finance and investment and appear regularly in the *Financial Times*, *Shares*, *International Fund Investment*, and on the Ample Interactive Investor website. He also edits the *Zurich Club Communique*, an investment newsletter.

He has written several other books about investing, covering topics such as online investing, venture capital and hedge funds, including *First Steps in Shares*, *First Steps in Bonds*, and *Traded Options*, all published by FT Prentice Hall.

He and his wife live near Kendal, in Cumbria, and have two grown-up children.

Acknowledgements

Over many years I have talked to a number of economists and economic statisticians about the way economic numbers fit into our daily lives. This book presents me with an opportunity to remember and thank them for the input.

In no particular order they are Derek Bagshaw (who introduced me to the subject), Professor Peter Sadler, and former colleagues from the City – Roger Nightingale, Richard Jeffrey and the late Alan Butler Henderson.

Professor Tim Congdon at Lombard Street Research spared a generous amount of his valuable time to assist me in understanding how forecasters go about their work.

National Statistics is a hugely valuable resource for anyone wanting to study and write about economic statistics in the UK. Its releases each month of a range of statistics provide a huge amount of detail about the numbers themselves and how they are collected.

At FT Prentice Hall, Jonathan Agbenyega first raised with me the idea of writing a book about statistics as part of the *First Steps . . .* series. He deserves credit for overcoming my initial misgivings, for making numerous suggestions about how the book should look and the material to be covered.

Finally, as ever, a big thank you to my wife Lynn. Lynn conducted a considerable amount of research and contributed a big chunk of the writing for the first three chapters of the book, particularly the sections related to web-based statistics resources. She was also actively involved in vetting the manuscript to make sure it didn't contain too much jargon.

Needless to say, any errors and omissions that remain are entirely my doing.

A note on data sources

This book uses a range of sources for the data given in the tables.

We have credited the source for the table in each case. The GDP statistics quoted in Chapter 2 are extracted from *The Pocket World in Figures*, 2001 edition, published by *The Economist*. This is an excellent book and contains a large amount of information on individual countries.

The website tables in chapters 2 and 3 have been compiled by inspecting the sites concerned. Most of the work on these chapters was done in the second half of 2001, although some have been checked more recently. Information on web sites inevitably dates faster than printed material, and readers are urged to visit the sites in question to verify the information for themselves. We have attempted to be as objective as possible in assessing the sites concerned, but ultimately the comments represent the personal views of the author.

The figures quoted in the sections on individual statistics from Chapter 4 onwards are predominantly extracted from publications produced by official sources, notably National Statistics and (for interest rates and monetary statistics) the Bank of England. Many tables have been updated at proof stage to make them as current as possible. Readers should note that data is frequently revised and should check the web sites of the organizations for the up-to-date position. The figures are shown for illustrative purposes only.

Considerably more data is provided in the official releases and these should be consulted wherever possible. Once again, though as up to date as possible, at the time of going to press, the figures quoted are inevitably some months old. Figures for the ratios and statistics in Chapter 10 are derived from a variety of sources, including the national press.

Contents

Introduction

This book is about statistics and what they can tell us about economics and financial markets. But before you put it down, imagining the subject will be dry and boring, think again.

All of us, whether or not we are active investors, need to understand all the forces that drive financial markets. Most people have a stake in these markets and the wider economy. It may be through their pension fund. It may be because they have savings and borrowings. Or it may be simply because their job depends on the health of the economy.

Economic statistics give us snapshots of how the economy is performing. Company profits are important. But at the root of financial market movements is the underlying health of the national and global economy. This is why the markets pay so much attention to the wide range of economic statistics. Every working day statistics are released that cover different aspects of economic performance in the big industrialized countries. These regular releases in the US, UK, Europe and Japan provoke widespread comment in the media.

It is easy to do down economic statistics and other market indicators. Benjamin Disraeli once commented that there were 'lies, damn lies, and statistics'. Interpreting statistics accurately is a skilled business, but not immune to the application of a little bit of common sense. The statistics themselves are open to abuse by the unscrupulous. Often they can be opaque. Statistics can be both a help and a hindrance to clarity of thought about the markets. And they can be presented in ways that are misleading.

> Statistics can be both a help and a hindrance to clarity of thought about the markets.

One simple example of this is the way financial news channels present the announcements of economic statistics. Frequently the published figures are compared with what economists at leading investment banks were expecting. Focusing on a single month's number compared with a consensus figure is OK as far as it goes. But it begs several questions:

- Is the consensus correct?
- How significant is one month's figure?
- Where does the number fit in the overall trend?
- Was it influenced by special factors?
- How accurate is it?
- Will it be revised at a later date?

The economists and strategists employed by investment banks and other commercial organizations often have a vested interest. Not in a particular statistical outcome, but simply in persuading investors to buy and sell more shares and bonds. This means there is a temptation to imbue individual figures with an importance they do not deserve. Often the figures need to be seen in the context of a longer-term trend. The conclusions to be drawn from one month or even several months' figures may be strictly limited. But commentators will rarely admit it. To do so would downgrade their importance as pundits.

Subsequent revisions to economic statistics, which may come several weeks later, rarely receive the same attention as the original 'flash' announcement. For all of these reasons, making snap judgements on the basis of a single number can be risky.

Nonetheless, however imperfect they may be, market indicators are important to investors. Why? The main reason is that they provide the economic context against which individual companies operate.

The change in consumer spending is a guide to how good or bad trading has been for retailers. Movements in the oil price affect not just oil companies but companies using their products, from chemical companies to bus operators. Changes in exchange rates affect companies with subsidiaries overseas or which buy from suppliers and sell to customers in foreign markets. Movements in interest rates have an impact on specific sections of the market (such as banks). They also affect companies with sizeable cash balances or heavy borrowings.

Movements in some market indicators are reckoned to be good predictors of future economic activity. These are the so-called leading indicators. Others are laggards and of interest only to economic historians and students of market cycles. So the numbers affect us all, whether or not we are investors. They reflect what is going on in our daily lives. Inflation hits hard those on fixed incomes. Unemployment statistics take on a new meaning for those who have been made redundant. They will be seeking work in competition with other job seekers. Periods of high unemployment and high inflation are unforgettable for those who have been their victims.

This is not a book for statisticians. I was trained 30-odd years ago as an economist and statistician. But in the course of writing this book I've had to take something of a refresher course to remember some of the lessons and techniques I'd long since forgotten. I made one discovery, though. It is this. All that interpreting economic statistics at the basic level requires is a reasonable degree of numeracy and a dose of common sense.

Some concepts – standard deviations, indices, regression analysis and correlations – are more complex. Yet with a little explanation non-statistics buffs can grasp what they mean. It's important not to be afraid of the numbers. Understanding what makes them tick is the important thing. And it can be rewarding.

> The rewards come from being able to place in context what the pundits spout, and sort the good information from the self-serving and misleading.

The rewards come from being able to place in context what the pundits spout, and sort the good information from the self-serving and misleading. There are also rewards from being able to make a more considered judgement for yourself about the significance of the numbers. Investment opportunities may arise by going against the herd when the market reacts incorrectly to a particular statistic or gives it an importance it does not merit. In other words, knowing what lies behind the numbers can give you the opportunity to make money.

How this book is organized

The first part of the book looks at economic statistics and other market indicators from the point of view of the old standbys used by journalists to write a story – what, who, when, where, why and how.

In turn the first three chapters examine the how, who and where:

■ How the numbers are calculated – where the data comes from, and the statistical techniques and concepts underlying the calculations.

■ Who collects the numbers – the statistics organizations around the world, including national statistics organizations, central banks and international bodies. Who forecasts the statistics – investment banks, independent forecasters and academics – and how good they are at it.

■ Where to find information on economic statistics and other market indicators, including media sources and the websites of statistics organizations.

The rest of the book covers the what, when and why part of the equation. This covers what the main statistics are and how they are calculated, when they are released, and why they might mean something for you.

Each of these chapters covers in more detail the individual statistics that are released regularly in all the main markets in six major groups: what we earn, save and borrow, including discussion of interest rates; prices and money; gross domestic product (GDP), consumption and government spending; production, output and employment; foreign trade; and a range of other important indicators.

Each of these chapters has several sections, looking at the individual statistics. As far as possible, each section describes the statistics in a standard way. It contains a description of the statistic or indicator, and shows how it has moved in recent years. It identifies the data used to calculate the number and how the information is collected. It describes what the numbers mean for investors and how they should be interpreted. And it looks at the drawbacks and inaccuracies that can cloud their meaning.

In each case we will also attempt to look at other differences: in definition, of different names, of different methods of calculation and collection. These sometimes occur between different major markets, whether the US, UK, Germany, France, Italy or Japan. We need to know what they are.

Are there ways in which the calculation and dissemination of statistics could be improved to bring greater clarity to the formulation of economic policy? I think so. If politicians rely unduly on out-of-date or inaccurate statistics, or don't know how to interpret them, the chances are they will make mistakes that affect us all.

How economic indicators are calculated

S tatistics aren't boring. They might sound as if they are. But market indicators – statistics on interest rates, gross domestic product (GDP), inflation, un employment – move share prices and bond markets. They are important to all of us in other ways too. Interest rates affect mortgages; inflation harms those on fixed incomes; rising unemployment might make you fear for job prospects.

Most measures of economic performance have implications for one or another part of our daily lives. Yet how many of us really understand how the figures are calculated? How many really know how to interpret them? And if we don't, should we strive to know more?

That we do not know or understand is partly the fault of the education system. There is little teaching of basic statistics, let alone the financial realities of life, in the mainstream curriculum. Many commentators make a good living out of describing and interpreting statistics. Often their comments are banal and trite. The pundit industry would collapse if we all knew more about these numbers and could judge them for ourselves.

So the purpose of this book is to try to explain more clearly how these market-moving indicators are compiled. The aim is also to look at what significance you should attach to them. This book will show you how to be wise to the bamboozlement and tosh offered by some commentators with an axe to grind. And it will show you how to avoid common traps in interpreting them for yourself.

Interpreting market indicators is a minefield. Many of these indicators are official statistics that relate to economic performance. Although official statistics are usually honestly compiled, their accuracy varies. And the message you take from them can be influenced by outside commentators' misleading presentation. Our ignorance of the ways in which they are compiled doesn't help.

So while you can trust up to a point the numbers published by a national statistical organization – like the UK's National Statistics – you need to be aware of the limitations of the numbers. This often comes from the way they are assembled.

The rest of this chapter covers some of the main ways in which statistics are compiled and presented, and some of the common ways in which they can be misinterpreted. But for an example of what we are all up against here, just think for a moment about one important statistic – the retail price index (RPI).

The RPI – an example

The RPI is the conventional way in which inflation is measured. It is an important number for several reasons. It influences many aspects of economic policy. Interest rate policy pays great attention to movements in the RPI, for example. But it affects people in other ways too. Some pensions are linked to it, wage demands may be set by reference to it, and so on.

Yet measuring changes in retail prices is an inexact science. It would be an impossible task for every small change in the retail prices of every item sold in every shop in every high street in the country to be measured every month. The UK's statisticians therefore use a large and carefully constructed sample to provide an approximation of the change in retail prices.

A sample is a small representative selection from a larger whole. Its characteristics – in this case changes in price – are measured. It is then assumed that the measurements of the sample are likely to be approximately the same for the whole. But in many senses that is all it is – an approximation. The problem with any sample is that it is impossible to be certain that the sample that has been taken is an accurate reflection of the whole (statisticians use the term 'population'). The paradox is that you can't really know whether the sample is accurate without knowing the exact characteristics of the 'population'. And if you know its characteristics, you have no use for the sample.

> The important point about sampling is that a sample by definition can contain some margin of error.

The important point about sampling is that a sample by definition can contain some margin of error. In the cases of the RPI the chances are that it is small, but it is there nonetheless.

There is another important point to make. Even if you assume that the RPI is precisely accurate to the nth degree, it is only accurate for an 'average' member of the population. The importance given to each item in the RPI – whether it is food, cigarettes, mortgage rates or petrol – is given a greater or lesser weight in the overall figure according to the spending patterns displayed by an annual survey of a typical family's spending.

But not everyone's spending confirms the average. My RPI will differ from yours. As a 53-year-old teetotal non-smoker with no dependent children, no mortgage and a modest annual mileage in my car, my inflation rate will be different from that of a family who smoke and drink, have two cars, three children to clothe and feed, and a mortgage.

This isn't the end of the problems entailed in interpreting the figures. Many commentators imbue monthly RPI figures with a significance they don't warrant. The change in RPI from one month to the next may or may not be significant. It may be influenced by unusual factors that applied only that month. Perhaps some abnormal weather influenced the price of one item in the index. Perhaps there was a sudden drop in the oil price. Perhaps mortgage rates fell that month. Perhaps all three happened together. In other words, deducing a trend from one month's figures can be dangerous. Although commentators usually trot this out as a caveat, it's normally only paying lip service.

Statistics can also be adjusted and manipulated. Sometimes the adjustments are helpful. In the case of the RPI, for example, seasonal adjustments can be made. These reduce or eliminate the effect of items that vary sharply in price at different times of the year. They smooth out the figures, giving a better view of a trend. A 'moving average' of several months' figures may give a better view of an underlying trend. But neither of these is a panacea when it comes to interpreting the numbers.

The less scrupulous might 'annualize' one month or one quarter's figures. We show later in the chapter how this calculation is done. But inappropriate annualizing can cause problems. If this month's figures are sharply at variance with last month's, then drawing conclusions from the annualized figure could be misleading.

Some statistics are prone to revision. This is less true of the RPI than of some others. Often it is the initial announcement that gets the most attention rather than the revision. In other words, the markets frequently pay most attention to the least accurate figure.

It's not my intention here to denigrate the work either of statisticians or of those who forecast or comment on the numbers. The media in general, and broadcast financial news channels in particular, are frequently more to blame for the undue emphasis they pay to 'one month's figures'. In turn, stock and bond market traders react instinctively to the number, rather than delving into what it really means. Superficial analysis of these isolated and sometimes inaccurate figures produces trends and theories that sometimes may move markets in entirely the wrong direction.

The next section looks at the key building blocks of the indicators that we will profile in more detail later in the book, and the mechanics of calculating them. It's worth knowing this in order to interpret the figures better.

A later section will look in more detail at the common pitfalls of interpretation and how commentators can, if they wish, manipulate the numbers to prove their point.

Building blocks

Understanding how statistics are compiled and presented is the first step to really understanding what they mean.

Several different statistical concepts and methods are used to arrive at the figures, including sampling, index numbers, averages of various types and seasonal adjustments. Unfortunately there may be other calculations to do too. When we interpret statistics, we often make use of other techniques. These include growth rate calculations of various types and estimating trends using the statistical techniques of regression and correlation. We might also make use of measures that show how widely dispersed or otherwise a series of numbers is from an average or a trend. The main measure used in this case is known as the 'standard deviation'.

Although these terms may be unfamiliar, they are all based around common sense.

- Index numbers are often used to reduce one or more sets of numbers to a common basis. They make comparisons easier.

- Averages are often used to smooth out erratic series of numbers to get a better view of an underlying trend.

- Seasonal adjustments are used to eliminate misleading variations that get in the way of identifying an underlying trend.

- With economic statistics, regression analysis is used to plot a trend with mathematical precision.

- Correlation is used to show the extent to which a movement in one variable tends to be accompanied by the movement in a second.

In all cases, how the calculations are performed is less important than understanding what the concepts mean.

S I D E B A R

Volume and value, real and nominal

News items about economics frequently mention words such as 'real' and 'nominal' when talking about particular statistics. But what's the significance?

There is a great division in the presentation of statistics between those that are based on units and those that are based on money value. Take a simple example. Oil is produced in units called barrels. Statistics of oil production measured in barrels are statistics that relate to volume. Only when you work out what price each barrel might have sold at in the market can you work out the money value of that production.

It goes further than this, in fact. Because the oil price is expressed in US dollars, the actual money value of a barrel of oil will differ from country to country, depending on how their currencies move relative to the US dollar. In fact, one reason for the decision by OPEC (the Organization of Petroleum Exporting Countries) in the early 1970s to quadruple the price of oil was that the inflation of the 1960s and the resulting fall in the value of the dollar had reduced the international purchasing power of the oil states in the Middle East and elsewhere.

In short, volume multiplied by price equals value.

The other facet of this is that, even though we may not be able to identify the presence of units of production in a statistic, we can eliminate the effects of price changes by adjusting the figures over time by the change in the general price level. This is called expressing the statistics 'at constant prices' or 'in real terms'.

Because it is made up of a large number of different figures, for example, GDP – a widely used measure of the overall size of an economy – is normally expressed only in money terms. But by 'deflating' it by the movement in the general level of prices over the same period, we get to a truer measure of the underlying growth rate of an economy.

To show how this works, let's assume money GDP increased by 5% in a year and the general level of prices rose by 3% over the same period. It's obvious that a part of the 5% increase will not have been due to any overall increase in wealth creation, but simply down to the fact that prices have risen.

In fact, adjusting for this is a good way of illustrating how numbers may not mean precisely what we think they do. The common assumption in this case might be that the growth in real terms was exactly 2% (5% minus 3%). The correct way of performing this calculation is actually to divide 105 by 103 and then subtract 100.

This gives the slightly different answer of 1.94%. In other words, if both variables started out from the common base of 100 at the beginning of the year, they would reach 105 and 103 respectively by the end of the year and the difference in their rates of increase is 101.94, not (as you might expect) 102.

The first of the statistical building blocks we need to look at is **sampling**. One of the best ways of imagining how samples work is to think of a bag of buttons. The bag contains red buttons and white buttons mixed together. We want to work out what proportion of red buttons there is in the bag.

We could do this by emptying out the bag and counting them all. But this would take time and would be boring. The other way is to take a selection of the buttons and count them and to use the proportions displayed by the buttons we select as a way of estimating the proportions in the whole bag.

If we take a couple of handfuls of buttons – say 50 in all – and count them, we might get 15 red and 35 white ones. If we put those back and scoop out a larger number – say 150 – we might get 50 red and 100 white. This shows a couple of things. One is that the results of different samples can be different from each other. The other is that the larger the sample, the more likely it is to approximate the characteristics of the whole.

It makes sense. Logically, successively larger and larger samples will eventually get to the point where they equal the whole. So an estimate based on a large sample is better than one based on a small one.

Sampling needs to avoid bias. It needs to be random. Otherwise expensive and embarrassing mistakes can be made. There is a classic example of this. It finds its way into all the textbooks on the subject. A supposedly random sample opinion of voters taken on polling day in the first post-war US presidential election predicted that Dewey would win, whereas the result went to Truman. The bias in the sample was tracked down to the fact that the poll was conducted by phone. Poorer voters, without phones, were more likely to vote for Truman – as the result showed.

The other point is that the sample may need to be tailored to the job in hand. In the case of the RPI example we used earlier, the sample is constructed – the statistical term is 'stratified' – so as to give due weight to the way different goods and services are purchased. If, for example, 20% of consumers buy their meat through a local butcher and 80% through a supermarket, the sample must be constructed to reflect that. Within each category, the sample should be random.

This idea leads on naturally to **weighting**. Taking once again the example of the RPI once the stratified random sample of price changes has come up with increases or decreases for each category, we cannot simply take an average of all the changes to arrive at the RPI number. The reason is that we don't spend an equal amount on each different item. In the case of the RPI the weighting given to each category is worked out from patterns of family spending that are surveyed each year. The more the average family spends on an item each year, the bigger will be the importance attached to a change in its price in the overall figures.

Table 1.1 gives a simple example of how using weightings affects the outcome. In this case the average is calculated by added up the changes (110 + 102 + 115 + 100 + 180) and dividing by 5. The weighted average is the sum of the weighted changes divided by 100.

What the weighted changes show is easy to deduce. The fact that food makes up 40% of spending means that the 2% price change there is accorded greater importance, while the 80% increase in the price of diamonds, which make up only 5% of spending, while not ignored, has much less influence on the outcome.

Weighting is important in a number of ways in a variety of statistics, as we will see later.

Next, we need to look at index numbers. Many statistics are presented in the form of an **index number**. Most investors will be familiar with stock market indices, but indices are used to present statistics as well because they make for easier interpretation.

Any series of numbers can be converted into an index. All that needs to be done is to choose a base period and then recalculate the numbers in other years by reference to this base. Take a series of numbers covering the value of widget production year by year over several years. Step one is to take a base year. The value in the base year is multiplied or divided by an amount that will convert it to 100. This is the conversion factor. Then all the other figures in the series are converted by applying the same factor.

How this works is shown in Table 1.2.

Table 1.1 Effect of weighting

Item	Price change (from 100)	Weight	Weighted change
Petrol	110	25	2750
Food	102	40	4080
Beer	115	15	1725
Mortgage	100	15	1500
Diamonds	180	5	900
Average	121.4	Weighted average	109.6

Table 1.2 Calculating an index of widget production

Year	1995	1996	1997	1998	1999	2000	2001
Value (£m)	59.6	63.5	87.1	75.2	75.4	86.0	90.1

Take the 1996 figure as the base year. Dividing all the figures by 63.5 (the 1996 value), multiplying by 100 and rounding to the nearest whole number produces the index number series as follows:

Index	94	100	137	118	119	135	142

You can probably see intuitively that these numbers are somewhat easier to work with. You know instantly, for example, that the value of widget production grew by 37% in 1997 and by a total of 42% between 1996 and 2001.

Because indices have no units, it's also easier both to combine and compare different indices than it is the figures that underlie them, which may differ considerably in value. We might, for example, want to compare movements in the price of gold and oil on a chart to see how they react to different external events. However, the price of oil is (at the time of writing) around $26 a barrel, while the price of gold is $309 an ounce. Reducing each of the price series to an index, each with same starting point, and then drawing a graph from that gives us a much easier way of comparing them.

Index numbers also allow one an easy means of combining figures for different time periods. Let's assume in the example above that there was previously an index started in 1990 for the value of widget production. We can combine this with the index created above in the way shown in Table 1.3.

In addition, different indices and other variables can be combined by giving different weights to each separate index to reflect their relative importance. One of the obvious places where this happens is with stock market indices. We'll look at this in more detail in a later chapter, but bear in mind, for example, that indices such as the FTSE 100 index of leading UK shares measure the movement in the overall market value of the companies concerned. In other words, the changes in share prices are weighted by the company's size in terms of its total stock market value.

The concepts of weighting and the creation of stock market indices lead on to the idea of an **average**, another key statistical building block.

This means that 1% movement in the share price of BP or GlaxoSmithKline, which have a market value of more than £100bn at the time of writing, has four times the impact on the index as the same movement in the price of Barclays or HBOS, which are capitalized at £25bn.

The concepts of weighting and the creation of stock market indices lead on to the idea of an **average**, another key statistical building block.

Table 1.3 Rebasing index numbers

Year	1990	1991	1992	1993	1994	1995	1996	1997	1998
Old index	100	105	108	119	121	131			
New index						94	100	137	118 etc.

If 131 on the old index equals 94 on the new one, we can combine the two indices by multiplying all the preceding numbers by 94/131, or 0.7176. This produces:

Combined	72	75	78	85	87	94	100	137	118

Like many statistical terms the concept of an average is often misused. Statisticians generally call the average the 'mean'. Most people with a modicum of numeracy would calculate an average simply by adding up a series of values and dividing by the number in the series. The average of 3, 4, 5 and 6 is 4.5 (3 + 4 + 5 + 6, or 18, divided by 4). In strict statistical terms this is actually called the 'arithmetic mean'.

There is another way of calculating an average from these numbers, known as the 'geometric mean'. You calculate this by multiplying all the values together and take the appropriate root for the number of values. In the example in the previous paragraph, the geometric mean is the 4th root of 360 (3 × 4 × 5 × 6), which is actually 4.36, not 4.5.

Some stock exchange indices have been based around geometric means, but they have a drawback. This is the mathematical rule that the product of any series of numbers that includes zero is itself zero. Hence if any constituent of a stock market index constructed on geometric lines goes bust (and hence has a value of zero), the value of the index would theoretically be zero. If the FTSE 100 index had been calculated in this way when Railtrack (the company responsible for Britain's railway infrastructure) went into administration, there might have been even more explaining to do.

Back in the world of economic statistics and other market indicators, averages tend to be used in a relatively limited way. Often it is to try to assess the significance of one month's figures in the context of the average of a number of preceding months. Alternatively, it may be to assess, say, one country's GDP growth rate in the context of an average of its main competitors.

Let's take this second instance as an example. Table 1.4 shows imaginary GDP growth rates for several leading economies, together with their relative size. The numbers are simplified to make the point.

There are several ways of calculating what 'average' GDP growth might be, some valid and some not. We might, for example, just add the percentage changes together (as they are presented in the table) and divide by 4 to get an average growth rate of 0.375%. In fact, the strictly correct way of averaging percentage changes is to add 100 to the number before performing

Table 1.4 Average GDP growth

Country	Expected GDP growth (%)	GDP (in $bn)
US	1	8000
UK	0.5	1250
Japan	−1	4000
Germany	1	2000

the average. In other words, the average of the four growth rates is 101 + 100.5 + 99 + 101, or 401.5, divided by 4. In this specific example, it makes no difference, but in some cases it might.

If the purpose of the exercise is to compare the UK with the rest, a better idea might be to isolate the UK and average the growth of the other three countries. This produces an average growth of 0.33%, not 0.375%, making the UK's performance stand out a little more.

An even better comparison would be gained by weighting the average by the size of the country's GDP – in other words, giving twice as much importance to the USA's 1% growth rate as to Japan's decrease of 1%, which in turn would have doubled the weight of Germany's growth rate. In this instance – simplifying the calculation by omitting the thousands – we would add 8 times 101, 4 times 99, and 2 times 101, and then divide by the total of the weights. This produces 808 + 396 + 202, or 1406, which, divided by 14 (the total of the weights), gives a result of 100.43, or growth of 0.43%.

The point of the exercise is to show that calculating the average in three different ways, all equally valid, produces three different results.

If we just eyeball the figures we can also perhaps deduce that whatever figure we choose might be misleading. You could write the headline 'Britain's growth the best of world's major economies' or 'Britain's growth worst of major Western economies' and be right in both cases. Which headline you write might depend on the point you wanted to prove.

Table 1.5 An example of a moving average

Year	Quarter	Index	Four-quarter moving average
1999	Q1	100	
	Q2	105	
	Q3	107	
	Q4	108	105
2000	Q1	104	106
	Q2	103	105.5
	Q3	101	104
	Q4	105	103.3
2001	Q1	110	104.8
	Q2	115	107.8
	Q3	116	111.5
	Q4	114	113.8

A good way of comparing the latest in a sequence of statistics with what has gone before is to use what is known as a **moving average**. We can see how this works by using an example, as in Table 1.5.

The calculation needs some explanation. The moving average for the quarter is the total of that quarter's figure and the preceding three, divided by 4. In each case, as the calculation progresses, the latest month is added and the 'oldest' month is dropped.

A quick way of doing the calculation in succeeding months is to add (or subtract) from the latest figure the difference (which may be negative) divided by 4 between the latest quarter's figure and the one being dropped.

In the case of Q4 2001, for example, 114 is the latest actual number, 105 (the Q4 2000 figure) is being dropped. The difference between the two numbers is +9. So 2.3 (9/4, 2.25, or 2.3 rounded to one decimal place) is added to the moving average value for the previous quarter, which was 111.5. Thus by adding 111.5 and 2.3 we arrive at the moving average for the latest quarter of 113.8.

Comparing the sequence of underlying numbers and the moving average shows that the movement in the average is smoother than the changes in the underlying figures. Whether or not one can use moving averages to make predictions is a matter for some debate. Predictive power is sometimes claimed for moving averages of share prices. But in the case of economic statistics, moving averages are best used simply to put the latest month's number in some sort of perspective.

While working from underlying figures is usually better than working from derivations of them, there are cases where we might need to make an adjustment. This is because not to do so would be even more misleading. One instance of this is that many aspects of economic activity have a seasonal bias. Retail sales are heavier in the run-up to Christmas, for example. Construction activity is lighter in January and February when the weather is inhospitable. Attempts to adjust for these factors are called **seasonal adjustments**.

Often these will be based on adjusting raw data to conform to patterns that have been established over long periods of time. If December sales of menswear have typically been 125% of the monthly average, perhaps because of Christmas present buying, dividing the statistic for that month by 1.25 will produce a number that is in theory a truer comparison with those of previous and subsequent months – assuming these have also been adjusted in a similar way to offset their own particular seasonal bias.

It doesn't take a genius to see that adjustments like this can produce inaccuracies and that seasonally adjusted figures may need to be treated with a greater than normal pinch of salt. Adjustments may also need to be made to some statistics for the differing timing of public holidays. Equally, seasonally adjusted figures may either reduce or exaggerate the impact of factors that have nothing whatever to do with the seasons, such as a strike or a marked change in interest rates.

Averages are one means of finding what we might call the central tendency of a group of measurements. In the example earlier we look for the average growth in GDP of a group of countries. Another way of using it would be to find the average percentage gain or loss experienced by several different unit trusts. By working out the average, we can learn whether the fund in which we invested has done better or worse than the average.

S I D E B A R

Calculating standard deviation

Take five investment funds whose annual percentage performance is as follows:

6.2   6.5   8.3   9.2   9.5

The average is 7.9.
The deviations from the average in each case respectively are:

−1.7   −1.4   0.4   1.3   1.6

The squares of the deviations respectively are:

2.89   1.96   0.16   1.69   2.56

The variance (the average of the squared deviations) is 1.85
Standard deviation is the square root of the variance = square root of 1.73 = 1.36

Another interesting statistic, however, measures how widely a group of measurements – say unit trust performance figures – is dispersed, i.e. how widely or otherwise they differ from the average. This is measured by a statistical calculation called the **standard deviation**. The standard deviation is fairly easy to work out for small groups of numbers. For larger amounts of data it may be easier to use the functions in a spreadsheet or financial calculator.

The procedure for calculating a standard deviation can be reduced to several steps. Work out the arithmetic average of your group of values. Subtract the average from each value to get a series of 'deviations'. Work out the square of each deviation. Add them up and divide by the number of values. The resulting figure is known as the variance. The square root of the variance is the standard deviation.

Standard deviation is often used to compare different sets of numbers. One application from the investment sphere might be, for example, to compare the performance over the course of several weeks of two different types of investment. By the end of, say, a six-month period both have risen by the same percentage amount, but one has risen in a relatively smooth upward path while the other has traced an erratic zigzag motion. You would only be human if you opted for the one that showed the smoother path. Intuitively it is easy to see that this would have a lower standard deviation than the one that took the zigzag path to reach the same end result.

In the context of measuring and comparing share price and fund performances, standard deviation is related to volatility. In turn volatility is usually held to equate to risk. The more volatile a share or a fund, the greater the likelihood of you having to sell at a loss, and therefore the greater risk.

Finally, many economic and stock market indicators are expressed in terms of **growth rates**. We have used some of them in the earlier examples. But growth is a somewhat fluid term and we need to be sure that we are comparing like with like when using it.

Growth rates can be used, for example, which:

■ compare one month with the same month of the previous year

■ compare one year's total with the previous year's total

> The more volatile a share or a fund, the greater the likelihood of you having to sell at a loss, and therefore the greater risk.

Table 1.6 Monthly widget production (m)

Month	1999	2000	2001
January	53	60	72
February	51	62	71
March	60	73	85
April	61	72	75
May	72	80	
June	72	75	
July	73	74	
August	56	60	
September	60	61	
October	62	63	
November	61	61	
December	30	45	
Total	711	786	

■ compare the end of the last complete year with the end of the prior year

■ compare the current month with the figure at the end of the previous year

■ estimate what growth would be if the present month's growth rate held true for the succeeding 11 months.

Convention, custom and practice often dictate which type of growth rate is used. But the results can be very different depending on the choice you make.

In the examples in Table 1.6, the growth rates differ widely depending on which convention you use.

The annual change is 10.5% (from 711 to 786). In the first four months of 2001 for which there are figures, the growth rate has been 20%, 14.5%, 16.4% and 4.2%. The average of these growth rates is 13.8%. Prior to the latest month the cumulative production for the previous 12 months was 819m units and the cumulative production for that month and the preceding 11 was 822m, giving monthly year-on-year growth of 0.366%. On an annual-ized basis this growth rate would be 4.4%.

Which of these various figures – 10.5%, 13.8% or 4.4% – gives the most accurate explanation? Any of them could be spouted by a commentator or used in a newspaper headline.

As an aside, annualizing growth rates is particularly dangerous. Not only does it give undue emphasis to one month's figures, but also it is often thought, incorrectly, that simply multiplying one month's growth rate by 12 will produce the annualized figure.

In fact, the correct way to annualize one month's figure is to take the numerical expression of the growth rate (in this case 100.366) and raise it to the power of 12. This can be done using the y^x function on a financial calculator.

Pitfalls

This brings us on to some common pitfalls in interpreting statistics and things to watch out for when we are listening to pundits pontificate about them.

There is very possibly no unique way to interpret different sets of statistics correctly. In the case of one set of figures, different aspects of the number may need watching and the pitfalls that we can fall into might differ, too. Later in this book, as we look at the different types of statistics, we will highlight some of the ways you can avoid misinterpreting them.

However, there are a few general questions we need to ask ourselves each time we are confronted with statistics.

■ Is the source impeccable?

■ Is it based on a sample or the whole?

■ Is it fact or opinion?

■ What period does it cover?

■ Are there special factors?

■ Have any adjustments been made (say, for inflation or seasonal factors)?

■ How are growth rates based on the figures calculated?

■ Are the deductions we make from the figures reasonable ones?

We've covered some of these issues already. It almost goes without saying, for example, that figures produced by a national statistics organization or a central bank in the country concerned are probably about as reliable as they can be.

Statistics from trade associations can be useful. In the US, for example, one widely watched number is the figure for wholesale prices from the Institute for Supply Management (ISM). The ISM number is generally considered to be accurate. But the limitations on figures like this in general are on the extent to which it is voluntary for contributing organizations to supply the figures and if only a proportion of those sampled comply, the extent to which the sample remains a meaningful one is affected.

The fact that many statistics are based on samples ought to be a caution against placing undue reliance on them. The size and construction of the sample is a key variable in the overall accuracy or otherwise of the indicator produced by it.

A more potent distinction is the difference between fact and opinion. While doubtless scientifically constructed, the fact is that statistics on consumer confidence and business confidence are expressions of opinion rather than fact. However accurate is the polling and sampling and however objective the questioning, the fact remains that public opinion is fickle.

Cynics sometimes say that the stock market itself is the best indicator of consumer confidence, although whether one should rely on it as such is perhaps open to question.

Let's look at some of these issues in turn.

It is pretty well known that the message conveyed by statistics can be manipulated by a judicious choice of starting and ending point. In their advertising, fund management groups have been known, for example, to choose a period over which to measure their performance, so as to put it in a more attractive light. So much so, in fact, that stock market regulators are trying to put an end to this practice.

Monthly figures and the growth rates calculated on the back of them can be influenced by special factors such as leads and lags in shipments, the incidence of public holidays, the number of weekends falling in the month, strikes and other factors. Before drawing conclusions, particularly if the figures show something wholly unexpected, we need to examine whether special factors might have influenced the numbers.

Adjustments are sometimes made to official statistics. Common ones are those that strip out seasonal variations and those that adjust for the effects of inflation. We need to be aware of whether or not these adjustments are present and how influential they might be in the overall scheme of things.

Another type of adjustment is that statistics are frequently revised, sometimes by a significant amount, often some time after the event. New information comes to light, missing figures are supplied, a more complete sample is obtained and the result is that the number may differ from the one originally released. Often several revisions are made. It is invariably the case that the stock market pays much less attention to the more accurate, revised figure issued later than it does to the less accurate one released first. That said, subsequent forecasts would probably be revised to take account of the changed number.

As the previous section demonstrates, there are several ways in which growth rates and other variables can be stated that are essentially a matter of personal choice. We need to be clear which ones a particular commentator is using and that the interpretation based on it is valid. It's generally better to rely on interpreting a trend rather than a single month's figure. Drawing conclusions based on annualizing one month's figures is particularly suspect.

Finally, we need to be careful about the conclusions we draw and the assumptions we make about statistical relationships. One common technique used when comparing different sets of statistics is correlation and regression. Correlation concerns the strength of relationships between two sets of numbers. Regression analysis measures the precise nature of the relationship and allows one to make predictions.

But, as statisticians are always taught at a very early stage in their careers, one needs to beware of moving from the fact that two variables exhibit a strong correlation to making the assumption that there is some sort of cause and effect relationship between them. There may be an unmeasured third variable that better explains the link between the other two.

If there is a strong correlation between areas where the divorce rate is high and the incidence of cirrhosis of the liver, it does not make sense to say that a divorce in itself causes the disease. It is more likely that the divorce is either caused by or precipitates heavy alcohol consumption, which in turn causes the disease. A strong correlation is not evidence of a direct causal relationship.

As we go through the book, we'll refer from time to time to some of the ideas outlined in this chapter. If you need to refer back, do so. It might make sense to reread this chapter before going on to the next.

The next chapter looks at the organizations responsible for collecting and publishing official statistics and where to go for the information they provide.

IN BRIEF

■ Statistics are valuable indicators but cannot be wholly trusted.

■ Sampling needs to be random and stratified to avoid errors.

■ Converting figures to indices makes for easier interpretation.

■ Averages are used to find the central tendency of a group of measurements and can be calculated in several ways.

■ Standard deviation is a measure of how widely a set of variables is dispersed from their average.

■ Growth rates can be calculated in different ways, but should aim to compare like with like.

Who collects and issues them?

Markets usually rely on economic and financial statistics to be accurate. They often make the brave assumption that they are so. But the quality of economic and financial statistics varies considerably from country to country. Often they are collected and published by different organizations in different countries.

Even within single countries, the organization of statistics collection varies considerably. Statistics are also produced by international organizations. On occasion they may either reinforce or contradict those produced nationally. Some widely watched statistics are produced by market research organizations, trade associations or other independent entities.

On its own this should not create huge problems. Statistics are calculated according to precise methods. All professional statisticians should adhere to them. In other words, there is no intrinsic reason to assume that statisticians in Slovenia pursue their calling any less diligently than those in, say, Sweden. Or to assume that the figures assembled by the Organization for Economic Cooperation and Development (OECD) are any less accurate than those of the countries that comprise it. Or to feel that the figures produced by the ISM in the US are of a different standard to those of the IFO in Germany.

These different approaches to the collection and publishing of statistical information simply make it more difficult for researchers and forecasters to find the information they need.

S I D E B A R

US statistics not as perfect as they appear

Even in the world's largest economy there can be problems. In the US, the publication of financial market statistics is the responsibility of the Federal Reserve, the US central bank. Other organizations collect more workaday statistics. These include Fedstats, Stat-USA, the US Census Bureau, and several other federal bodies.

Successive administrations have made attempts to collate the important statistics into a coherent whole. In the Clinton era, for example, the White House operated two separate 'briefing rooms' on the web, for financial statistics and economic statistics.

Such clarity of purpose is rare. US statistics can be something of a patchwork between data that is collected at federal level and that produced at state level. Many different entities are involved.

For all its free market 'small government' rhetoric, the US is a bigger bureaucracy than is often supposed. So can we be sure that all of the statistics collected, for example at state and local level, are as accurate as those, say, assembled by the Fed? Sadly, the answer may be 'no'.

In many countries, the division of labour between statistics organizations is sometimes more straightforward than it is in the US. Statistics are often collected just by a national statistical office (such as the UK's National Statistics) and by a central bank (like the Bank of England).

Frequently the central bank collects and publishes statistics relating to monetary policy and the operation of financial markets. The national statistics organization collects, collates and publishes all the rest. In other markets, the national statistics organization does it all. In some instances the precise division of responsibility differs.

But there are complications. In the EU, and especially within the Euro-zone – the 12 countries that now use the Euro as their national currency – things are different. Here, as well as statistics published nationally by member states, there is an overlay of statistics collected and published by EU organizations such as Eurostat. Eurostat serves as the 'national' statistics organization of the EU.

SIDEBAR

European statistics – lack of consistency

Analyzing EU economic and financial performance on a consistent basis can be tricky.

One reason is that economic statistics collected by Eurostat cover the 15 EU member states. By contrast, the European Central Bank (ECB), which sets monetary policy for the 12 Euro-zone economies, collects and produces statistics related to the financial economy, financial markets and the monetary function for which it is responsible. In other words, monetary statistics cover 12 countries; the other statistics cover 15.

Because they include those countries that are not members of the Euro-zone but which nonetheless are EU members, the Eurostat figures are more representative of economic activity in the EU than the ECB figures are of monetary activity in the whole union.

This isn't so bad, as it turns out. Forecasters and commentators can always get the required numbers from somewhere. At the time of writing, individual central banks within Euro-zone countries were also still producing monetary statistics for their individual national markets. It is, though, quite conceivable that this function may shrink and eventually die. It is not so much that the figures won't be produced, but more that they may go largely unnoticed.

How quickly this happens probably depends in some measure on the confidence that analysts and commentators have in the ability and willingness of the ECB to commit to publishing data that splits out (statisticians use the jargon 'disaggregate' for this process) the performance of individual countries.

Even then, you might draw a comparison with the US. Few commentators are interested in the economic activity of individual states, only of America as a whole. Might the same eventually be true of the EU?

In the wider sense, though countries' statisticians pursue their calling with professional zeal, in some cases the comparison of the same statistics between countries can be difficult. Comparing China with the US, for example, or Italy with Iceland might be tricky.

One reason for this is that the nature of a country and the work done by people within it may place obstacles in the way of efficient collection and calculation of statistics. Big countries with populations concentrated in cities and business activity conducted by companies and the public sector make easier subjects. It's harder where the activity is mainly in agriculture and the population is spread over wide areas. In farming economies, for example, more transactions may be for cash or even go unrecorded. Work on the family farm may not be paid in the form of conventional wage, but it is economic activity nonetheless. Even in some western economies, the size of the 'black economy' – illicit activities or those where services are performed for cash to evade tax – may distort comparisons.

Even the degree to which women have jobs can have an effect on the numbers – hence the calculations sometimes reported in the press that cost out the economic value of a housewife.

In some cases, even where accurate statistics can be produced, there are differences between countries in the speed with which the raw data is collected and

Bigger countries and those with a more diverse industrial base may take longer to collect and publish statistics.

the statistics collated. Bigger countries and those with a more diverse industrial base may take longer to collect and publish statistics. Indonesia will probably find it takes longer to collect and collate its statistics than Ireland.

Sometimes, there are variations that are down to differences in interpretation of data.

In the *Pocket World in Figures*, a useful guide produced by *The Economist*, the authors note that 'the extent and quality of the statistics available vary from country to country ... figures from individual countries will often differ from standard international statistical definitions.'

Who's who in international and national statistics

The situation within the EU – where there are 15 member states but only 12 'monetary' members – highlights one of the more confusing aspects of the statistics game.

There are several tiers of organization that function, either formally or informally, as statistics-gatherers, or whose statistical performance is often commented on collectively or individually in the press. Examining the different tiers helps one understand the relative size of different countries within the world economy and the size of some of the international groupings.

Table 2.1 gives an indication of the rough order of size of the biggest economies in the world as measured by their GDP in US dollars. GDP is more or less the standard way of measuring a country's economic size. It is the value of all the output of goods and services produced within a country.

The most obvious point from the table is the sheer size and importance of the US economy. On its own it accounts for just over 20% of the world economy. It is roughly twice the size of the next biggest (Japan). And it accounts for close to 40% of the combined GDP of the 28 countries that the International Monetary Fund (IMF) calls 'advanced' countries.

Another point is that many internationally traded commodities – the most important of which is undoubtedly oil – are denominated and traded in terms of the US dollar. Several countries, notably some in Latin America, have their currencies pegged to the value of the dollar.

The most frequently mentioned international groups for which statistics are separately produced, or on which comments are made about individual members' economic and financial performance, are the G7 group of advanced industrial countries and the OECD. The latter has 29 members. Based in Paris, it produces a range of statistics. These include figures that tot up the individual statistics of all its member countries. The G7 is a less formal grouping. It is more akin to a political and economic club rather than a specific organization.

In a political sense the G7 has been expanded to the G8, to include Russia, although Russia would not normally be considered on a par with G7 members in economic terms (see Table 2.2). Its GDP is some $330bn. This places it between Mexico and Argentina in terms of economic clout. Its economy is, for example, around a third the size of China's.

The OECD, by contrast, comprises the main industrial countries (23 in all), plus the Czech Republic, Hungary, Mexico, Poland, South Korea and Turkey. The 23 industrial countries are, by a conventional definition first established by the IMF, the 15 current EU members plus Australia, Canada, Iceland, Japan, New Zealand, Norway, Switzerland and the US.

Table 2.1 1998 Top 20 economies by $GDP

Country	GDP ($bn)	Country	GDP ($bn)
US	7903	India	427
Japan	4089	South Korea	399
Germany	2180	Netherlands	389
France	1465	Australia	387
UK	1264	Mexico	368
Italy	1157	Russia	332
China	924	Argentina	290
Brazil	768	Switzerland	284
Canada	581	Taiwan	262
Spain	555	Belgium	259
		Total of top 20	**24283**

Source: The Economist

Table 2.2 1998 GDP of G8 countries

Country	GDP ($bn)
US	7903
Japan	4089
Germany	2180
France	1465
UK	1264
Italy	1157
Canada	581
Russia	332
Total of G8	**18971**

Source: The Economist

Since the advent of the Euro and a common monetary policy and increasingly synchronized economies, the EU and Euro-zone have become important groups in their own right, especially by comparison with the US. The wider EU's GDP is approximately the same size as that of the US. It is just short of 20% of the world total.

For the record, the EU comprises Austria, Belgium, Denmark, Finland, France, Germany, Greece, Ireland, Italy, Luxembourg, the Netherlands, Portugal, Spain, Sweden and the UK. The Euro-zone is made up of 12 of this list, but excludes Denmark, Sweden and the UK. For the record too, neither Switzerland nor Norway are EU members.

Table 2.3 shows the relative size of the EU members in terms of their dollar GDP.

There are other groups and definitions used. The Schengen group is a political grouping within the EU that has abolished border controls. Its members were originally the Benelux countries and France and Germany, but the group has since been expanded to include all of the Continental European EU members, with the exception of Greece.

Newly industrialized Asian countries (defined as Singapore, Hong Kong, South Korea and Taiwan) and Israel are sometimes included with the 23 industrial countries mentioned earlier. These are collectively dubbed 'advanced' countries.

Table 2.3 1998 GDP of EU countries

Country	GDP ($bn)
Austria	217
Belgium	259
Denmark	175
Finland	125
France	1465
Germany	2180
Greece	123
Ireland	69
Italy	1157
Netherlands	389
Portugal	106
Spain	555
Sweden	227
UK	1264
Luxembourg	19
Total of EU 15	8330

Source: The Economist

The final important group, from a statistical and economic policy standpoint, are the oil-exporting countries of OPEC. This grouping has 12 members. They are Algeria, Gabon, Indonesia, Iran, Iraq, Kuwait, Libya, Nigeria, Qatar, Saudi Arabia, the United Arab Emirates (UAE) and Venezuela. Table 2.4 shows the relative size of these countries in GDP terms. As befits its pivotal role as the custodian of a large part of the world's oil, OPEC produces a range of statistical publications. These include a monthly oil bulletin and an annual statistical report.

Table 2.5 show the names and web addresses of the national statistical organizations of the main countries mentioned earlier, together with the country name.

Most national statistics organizations are agencies of their government. As such they are publicly funded and staffed by civil servants. The quality of the data produced to some degree depends on the number of staff employed relative to the amount of statistical information they are expected to produce.

One characteristic of organizations like this and the websites and print publications they provide is obvious in a way. It is that they tend to reflect the country's national characteristics, not unlike a state airline. Indeed, having a national statistics organization seems to be viewed, like having an airline, as part of being a nation state. This is irrespective of whether or not the country concerned has or can collect and collate any statistics worthy of the name.

The efficiency with which data is displayed on the web or in print frequently reflects national predilections for design. Design quirks sometimes get in the way of interpreting the data. Most users of statistics prefer websites like this to have a range of key attributes. These include clean design with few gimmicks, well-sourced data with detailed descriptions of how the figures are arrived at, any special factors involved in a particular statistical series, and contact names of individuals who can be approached if further questions are necessary.

Table 2.4 GDP of OPEC countries

Country	GDP ($bn)
Saudi Arabia	143
Indonesia	131
Iran	102
Venezuela	82
UAE	49
Others (7)	c.93
Approximate total	600

Source: The Economist

Table 2.5 National statistical organizations

Organization	URL	Country
Algeria ONS	www.ons.dz	Algeria
INDEC	www.indec.mecon.ar	Argentina
Australian Bureau of Statistics	www.abs.gov.au	Australia
OSZ	www.oestat.gv.at	Austria
Azeristat	www.azeri.com/goscomstat	Azerbaijan
Bangladesh	www.bangladeshgov.org	Bangladesh
Ministry of Stats	president.gov.by/Minstat/	Belarus
Statistics Belgium	www.statbel.fgov.be	Belgium
INE	www.ine.gov.bo	Bolivia
IBGE	www.ibge.gov.br	Brazil
NSI	www.nsi.bg	Bulgaria
Statistics Canada	www.statcan.ca	Canada
INE	actualidad.araucania.cl/ine	Chile
China	www.stats.gov.cn	China
Hong Kong/China	www.info.gov.hk/censtatd	China
DANE	www.dane.gov.co	Colombia
CroStat	www.dzs.hr	Croatia
Cyprus OSR	www.pio.gov.cy	Cyprus
Czech Republic CSU	www.czso.cz	Czech Republic
Statistics Denmark	www.dst.dk	Denmark
INEC	www.inec.gov.ec	Ecuador
Egypt Ministry of Economy	www.capmas.gov.eg	Egypt
Eire CSO	www.cso.ie	Eire
Estonia Statistikaamet	www.stat.ee	Estonia
Eurostat	www.europa.eu.int	Europe
Statistics Finland	www.stat.fi	Finland
INSEE (France)	www.insee.fr	France
Federal Statistics Office	www.statistik-bund.de	Germany
Greece	www.statistics.gr	Greece
Guatemala	sever.rds.org.gt	Guatemala
HCSO	www.ksh.hu	Hungary
Statistics Iceland	www.statice.is/english	Iceland
DOS	www.nic.in/stat	India
BPS	www.bps.go.id	Indonesia
Israel CBS	www.cbs.gov.il	Israel
ISTAT	www.istat.it	Italy
JSB	www.stat.go.jp	Japan
Jordan CBJ	www.cbj.gov.jo	Jordan
Kazstat	www.kazstst.asdc.kz	Kazakhstan

Organization	URL	Country
CSB	www.csb.lv	Latvia
Statistics Lithuania	www.std.lt	Lithuania
STATEC	statec.gouvernement.lu	Luxembourg
DOS	www.statistics.gov.my	Malaysia
COS	www.nso.gov.mt	Malta
INEGI	www.inegi.gob.mx	Mexico
Statistics Netherlands	www.cbs.nl	Netherlands
Statistics New Zealand	www.stats.govt.nz	New Zealand
Statistics Norway	www.ssb.no	Norway
FBS Pakistan	www.statpak.gov.pk	Pakistan
Palestine PCBS	www.pcbs.org	Palestinian NA
INEI	www.inei.gob.pe	Peru
NSCB	www.nscb.gov.ph	Philippines
Poland PSP	www.stat.gov.pl	Poland
INE	www.ine.pt	Portugal
NCS	cns.kappa.ro	Romania
Goskomstat	www.gks.ru	Russia
Statistics S Africa	www.statssa.gov.za	S Africa
Statistics Singapore	www.singstat.gov.sg	Singapore
Slovak Statistics	www.statistics.sk	Slovakia
SUR (Slovenia)	www.sigov.si/zsr	Slovenia
South Korea	www.nso.go.kr/eng/	South Korea
Sweden SCB	www.scb.se	Sweden
Statistik Schweitz	www.staistik.admin.ch	Switzerland
Taiwan	www.dgbasey.gov.tw	Taiwan
Thailand	www.nso.go.th	Thailand
Turkey SIS	www.die.gov.tr	Turkey
UAE Ministry of Planning	www.uae.gov.ae/mop	UAE
European Central Bank	www.ecb.int	UK
Bank of England	www.bankofengland.co.uk	UK
Office of National Statistics	www.statistics.gov.uk	UK
Treasury	www.hm-treasury.gov.uk	UK
INE	www.ine.gub.uk	Uruguay
Bureau of Economic Analysis	www.bea.doc.gov	USA
Economic Statistics Briefing Room	www.whitehouse.gov.fsbr	USA
Fedstats	www.fedstats.gov	USA
Federal Reserve	www.federalreserve.gov	USA
OCEI	www.ocei.gov.ve	Venezuela
SZS	www.szs.sv.gov.yu	Yugoslavia (Serbia)

Source: www.linksitemoney.com

As outlined in the next section on national statistics and central banking websites, in some countries the statistics organizations discharge their obligations with admirable rigour and clarity. In other countries, however, the aims are more honoured in the breach.

Finally in the who's who, it is worth remembering that a number of closely watched statistics are compiled and published by organizations that are independent of government. Typically these are trade associations, employers' organizations, opinion pollsters and the like.

In the UK, for example, the Confederation of British Industry (CBI) and organizations like the Retail Consortium and the Society of Motor Manufacturers and Traders produce statistics. So do leading mortgage banks and other organizations. Some of these are covered in the next chapter.

Leaving this final aspect aside, however, official statistics can be looked on as objective. But more care needs to be taken with quasi-official statistics. These include those emanating from commercial organizations or those representing them, although this is not to belittle their contribution.

Let's take just one example. Halifax, the mortgage banking arm of leading UK banking group HBOS, has for many years produced a widely followed monthly survey of trends in the housing market. The statistics are based on activity at its branches. Similar punditry is practised by Nationwide, an independent mortgage bank. While no one suggests that their figures are inaccurate, they are sometimes contradictory and by definition cannot reflect entirely the precise composition of and trends in the whole market. Nonetheless they do provide general information and are closely watched by many.

One important point, however, is the need to watch the interpretation placed on monthly trends in the statistics emanating from commercial organizations. One reason is that they may – possibly unintentionally – be coloured by undue familiarity with the industry concerned. In other words, a more dispassionate observer, less closely involved with the industry, may be able to discern a bigger picture.

In addition to mortgage banks, retailers, car dealers and trade associations, there are several organizations, notably in the US, that produce market-moving statistics. One of the best known is the ISM (formerly the NAPM), which produces a monthly survey. The data is essentially an opinion poll on business confidence. It measures the movement in a range of variables affecting business, including production levels, new orders, stock levels and employment.

Other organizations within the US poll consumer confidence, also a key economic indicator much watched by the market.

The real question concerning these statistics echoes the concerns over all statistics related to economic performance. We can perhaps sum it up in a number of 'golden rules':

- Always prefer official statistics to privately produced ones.
- If using privately produced ones, scan the commentary for signs of bias.
- Always use revised statistics rather than flash numbers, if available.
- Always prefer fact-based statistics rather than opinion-based ones.
- Always prefer newer statistics to older ones.

Commentary on national statistics websites

Statistics information and commentary on newly published data are available from a variety of print-based sources. These are chiefly the quality end of the financial press, including the *Financial Times*, *The Wall Street Journal Europe*, *the Economist*, *Fortune*, *Business*, *Forbes* and similar publications.

National statistics organizations and central banks also produce statistics in print form. These usually include monthly bulletins and statistical yearbooks. Rarely are these available without charge. They don't come cheap either, but in many countries the relevant publications can be consulted in reference libraries. Have a look in a library in the UK, for example, for the *Monthly Digest of Statistics* or the *Annual Abstract of Statistics*.

The advent of the web has, however, revolutionized the distribution of this type of information. Most national statistics organizations have websites and many of them provide a wide range of statistical information.

SIDEBAR

Statistics websites and their attributes

All websites differ hugely in quality. What do statistics websites need to contain to satisfy users?

A key element in any site is ease of navigation. Overloading a site with highly detailed graphical content can leave the user frustrated because it slows down response time. A fancy home page with pretty pictures may look attractive when it eventually downloads, but a simple page listing the website contents is far more useful.

A sitemap covering the exact topics included on the site or for the site to be searchable are strong plus points. Surprisingly, many sites have no such facility and users can waste time trying to track down the relevant information.

A site needs to be intelligible. For all practical purposes this means having an English-language version. English is the common tongue of the web and not to have a version that can be read and understood by international users limits the use to which the site can be put. Most sites analyzed later in the chapter have an English version, although a few, notably those in South American countries, do not.

An important point for investors is whether or not a reasonable range of key indicators is present. In many sites, these are displayed prominently on the home page or are clearly linked to it. Common key indicators include the country's inflation rate, money supply statistics, GDP growth and so on. These should all be freely available at the site and should be updated month by month to be of any use.

Another strong plus point is whether the site indicates precisely when in the next few months, in terms of dates and times, key announcements of new data will be made. In the more prominent economies, data like this can be extremely important in determining the shorter-term movements in the market. To this end many sites have what is usually called an advance release calendar. This gives the important dates when key statistics will be released, so that forecasters can be prepared. On some sites this calendar is hidden away in the press release section and its presence is not immediately obvious from the home page.

Sites should usually contain news releases relating to key statistics and other matters. About one-third of the sites I looked at did not include this facility and some had releases only in the native language. Where they are available they are normally free, as is information regarding key economic highlights.

Other information is often available for a charge, whether it is in print form, CD Rom or PDF format. A rare few provide their publications free of charge if they are accessed online.

Finally, many sites allow users to e-mail statistics personnel with enquiries. This has obvious value for those wishing to delve into the figures. Many sites also have links to other statistics organizations worldwide or, in some instances, to business links in the country concerned.

I have analyzed around 80 national statistics organizations on this basis, itemizing their characteristics and scoring them on a consistent basis. This gives the sites 2 points for easy navigation (i.e. light graphical content), 1 point for medium and 0 for heavy graphics or obscure layout. I then give 1 point for each of the characteristics mentioned above. This gives a maximum score of 10 for a site.

It's not precise, but it's a good way of introducing some objectivity into measuring how good such sites are.

The key attributes for statistics websites can be summarized as:

- easy navigation

- sitemap

- searchable

- English version

- key indicators table
- advance release calendar
- news releases
- publications
- e-mail contact

How did the sites fare? Before looking in detail at them by region, it's worth highlighting a couple of general points. Intelligibility first. Of the European sites all have English versions with the exception of Austria. Remember, that the content of some sites is often not as comprehensive in English as it is in the native language. Some countries are still in the process of developing their English-language sites. These include Jordan, Bulgaria, China and Belgium.

Key indicators are available at most sites. At the time of writing, however, the information provided at some of the sites, such as Egypt and Bangladesh, was very out of date and of limited help to the average user.

Europe

Most European countries have a national statistics organization. This is true of the smallest Baltic state through to large countries like Germany and Russia. Large size does not necessarily equate to a good score, however.

Of the 30 sites I looked at, only one – that of the Netherlands – obtained a perfect score. Despite the advances made in website design, navigation is still a problem at some sites. Although there are quite a number of sites with commendably low graphical content and fast response times, some are needlessly convoluted and frustrating to use.

At the time of writing the worst offender is STATEC, the Luxembourg statistics organization. Yugoslavia is also extremely slow. It is sometimes hard to discover whether or not the slowness of the site is simply down to the design shortcomings or to the poor speed of the server.

All but seven of the sites include news releases as part of the information freely available. Of the remaining sites most have press releases in the native language only.

All the sites, with the exception of Bulgaria (which is still admittedly at the development stage), have a key indicators page. However, these are not always easy to find on sites lacking a sitemap. The Russian site, for example, has the information under 'database catalogue' – not the most obvious place any international user would choose to look.

Table 2.6 Top European sites

Organization	URL	Graphics	Advance release dates	Search/ sitemap	Press rele- ases	Key indic- ators	Publi- cations	Free?	E-mail contact	Links?	Score
Czech Republic CSU	www.czso.cz	Low	Yes	No	Yes	Yes	Yes	No	Yes	Yes	9
Statistics Denmark	www.dst.dk	Low	Yes	Yes	Yes	Yes	Yes	No	Yes	Yes	9
Estonia Statistikaamet	www.stat.ee	Low	Yes	Yes	Yes	Yes	Yes	No	Yes	Yes	9
Statistics Finland	www.stat.fi	Low	Yes	Yes	Yes	Yes	Yes	No	Yes	Yes	9
Eire CSO	www.cso.ie	Low	Yes	Yes	Yes	Yes	Yes	No	Yes	Yes	9
Statistics Lithuania	www.std.lt	Low	Yes	Yes	Yes	Yes	Yes	No	Yes	Yes	9
Statistics Netherlands	www.cbs.nl	Low	Yes	Yes	Yes	Yes	Yes	Yes	Yes	Yes	10
Statistics Norway	www.ssb.no	Low	Yes	Yes	Yes	Yes	Yes	No	Yes	Yes	9
Poland PSP	www.stat.gov.pl	Medium	Yes	Yes	Yes	Yes	Yes	Yes	Yes	Yes	9
Sweden SCB	www.scb.se	Low	Yes	Yes	Yes	Yes	Yes	No	Yes	Yes	9
Statistics Belgium	www.statbel.fgov.be	Low	Yes	Yes	No	Yes	Yes	Yes	Yes	Yes	9

Source: author; www.linksitemoney.com

All of the sites have details of publications available from the organization concerned. Publications in the English language are limited in some cases. Only a few select sites offer publications either substantially or wholly free: these are Estonia, the Netherlands, Belgium and Poland.

All of the sites except Hungary and Russia have links to other statistics organizations and general sites of interest, while all of the sites except Yugoslavia offer some form of e-mail contact.

Putting all this together, the best site among European statistics organizations looked at in this reasonably objective way is the Central Bureau of Statistics in the Netherlands, with Sweden, the Czech Republic, Estonia, Denmark, Finland, Eire, Lithuania, Norway and Belgium close behind (see Table 2.6).

The worst overall are Bulgaria, Yugoslavia and Slovenia. These sites are pretty devoid of content but obviously have some scope for improvement as they adjust further towards a market economy.

Among the interesting features of the sites are a link on the Netherlands site to 'Blaise', a programme developed by Statistics Netherlands for computer-assisted interviewing, data entry and data editing. Statline, the electronic databank of Statistics Netherlands, can be downloaded free of charge. Statistical information will soon be available in English on many subjects in the form of tables and graphs.

At the Danish site there are links to econometric models of the Danish economy, with the ability to access research papers and e-mail the statisticians involved. Much of the information is only available in Danish at the moment but an English abstract is provided for all papers. The Danish site overall is well designed and informative.

Many of the sites are very good and the criticisms are no more than quibbles that may not be particularly important to some investors and other users. For most major European economies a very reasonable amount of free information is available.

Asia and Australasia

Of the 19 Asian and Australasian sites looked at, by far the best is the Philippines. It records a perfect score. Australia, Malaysia and Singapore are not far behind, losing a point each because they do not offer free publications (see Table 2.7).

About half of the sites include advance release dates and all but three include up-to-date key financial indicators. In the case of Bangladesh, China and Azerbaijan, however, these are out of date.

Table 2.7 Top Asian sites

Organization	URL	Graphics	Advance release dates	Search/ sitemap	Press rele-ases	Key indic-ators	Publi-cations	Free?	E-mail contact	Links?	Country	Score
Australian Bureau of Statistics	www.abs.gov.au	Low	Yes	Yes	Yes	Yes	Yes	No	Yes	Yes	Australia	9
Hong Kong/China	www.info.gov.hk/censtatd	High	Yes	Yes	Yes	Yes	Yes	No	Yes	Yes	China	7
Statistics New Zealand	www.stats.govt.nz	Medium	Yes	Yes	Yes	Yes	Yes	No	Yes	Yes	New Zealand	8
NSCB	www.nscb.gov.ph	Low	Yes	Yes	Yes	Yes	Yes	Yes	Yes	Yes	Philippines	10
BPS	www.bps.go.id	Medium	No	Yes	Yes	Yes	Yes	No	Yes	Yes	Indonesia	7
DOS	www.statistics.gov.my	Low	Yes	Yes	Yes	Yes	Yes	No	Yes	Yes	Malaysia	9
Statistics Singapore	www.singstat.gov.sg	Low	Yes	Yes	Yes	Yes	Yes	No	Yes	Yes	Singapore	9
South Korea	www.nso.go.kr/eng/	Low	Yes	Yes	Yes	Yes	Yes	No	No	Yes	South Korea	8

Source: author: www.linksitemoney.com

Singapore has a new web-based data delivery service on its site – SingStat Express. This is free in some areas of the data, such as the monthly consumer price index.

South Korea has major indicators in chart form and news releases usefully indexed by subject. The sites on offer from Pakistan and India suffer from bad design.

Middle East and Africa

Of the sites on offer in the Middle East and Africa only South Africa recorded a perfect score. This is the only site to mention that web response times are usually slow at publication time of the key economic indicators. In what is an unusual service offering, it is possible to call a number at Statistics South Africa and an official will read the findings and fax extracts to the caller. The most recent publications on this site are in zip file format. The older ones are in PDF format. This and the Turkish site are the only two to offer advance release dates.

The Egyptian site operated by the Ministry of Economy has very little content and is out of date. South Africa and Jordan are the only two sites offering free publications but in the case of the latter some are only in Arabic.

Table 2.8 lists the Middle East and Africa sites.

The Americas

Outside the US the problem with the sites – especially those of South American countries – is the disinclination of many (with the exception of Brazil) to provide English versions. The Mexican site has publications in Spanish only.

Statistics Canada gets a perfect score with a site that is both easy to navigate and with all the required attributes. *The Daily* is Statistics Canada's official release bulletin and is released at 8.30 a.m. eastern time each working day. It contains news releases on the current social and economic conditions and announces new products. It has been posted on the web since June 1995. The site also offers 160 free publications and more than 35 free research papers.

Some information regarding Central and South American economies can be gleaned from the Inter-American Development Bank (**www.iadb.org**). The site contains news releases and research papers, most of which can be accessed in English. An interesting section contains 'Country Papers'. These include an overview of each individual country's current economic situation. There are also 'Country Economic Assessments', which are more detailed.

Table 2.8 Middle East and Africa sites

Organization	URL	Graphics	Advance release dates	Search/ sitemap	Press rele-ases	Key indic-ators	Publi-cations	Free?	E-mail contact	Links?	Country	Score
Algeria ONS	www.ons.dz	Medium	No	No	No	Yes	Yes	No	Yes	Yes	Algeria	5
Cyprus OSR	www.pio.gov.cy	Low	No	No	Yes	Yes	Yes	No	Yes	Yes	Cyprus	7
Egypt Ministry of Economy	www.capmas.gov.eg	Medium	No	No	No	No	No	No	No	No	Egypt	1
Israel CBS	www.cbs.gov.il	Medium	Yes	Yes	No	Yes	Yes	No	Yes	Yes	Israel	7
Jordan CBJ	www.dos.gov.jo	Low	No	No	Yes	Yes	Yes	No	Yes	Yes	Jordan	6
Palestine PCBS	www.pcbs.org	Medium	No	Yes	Yes	Yes	Yes	No	Yes	Yes	Palestinian NA	7
Statistics S Aafrica	www.statssa.gov.za	Low	Yes	Yes	Yes	Yes	Yes	Yes	Yes	Yes	S Africa	10
Turkey SIS	www.die.gov.tr	High	Yes	No	Yes	Yes	Yes	No	No	Yes	Turkey	5
UAE Ministry of Planning	www.uae.gov.ae/mop	Medium	No	Yes	No	Yes	No	No	Yes	Yes	UAE	5

Source: authors; www.linksitemoney.com

UK

This sub-section and the next two cover the official sources of information likely to be of most use to investors – namely those that cover the official sources of information relating to the UK and US economies, and statistics released centrally by the EU.

There are two key sources of information in the UK. One is National Statistics (formerly known as the Office for National Statistics and before that as the Central Statistical Office). Its web address is **www.statistics.gov.uk**. The other is the Treasury (**www.hm-treasury.gov.uk**).

The National Statistics' site offers a range of material including neighbourhood statistics, a new service. This offers users ready access to a vast range of local social and economic data, although it is expected to take a few years to reach its full implementation. The press release section is comprehensive and includes a searchable archive. The site also has access to a section called Statbase providing access to a wide range of government statistics. The standard format for data downloaded from Statbase is CSV, which can be read directly by many spreadsheet and other software packages. Another option is to download Navidata 3R, a software package designed and written by ONS. This allows users to work with time series data drawn from different sources and to manipulate and display them together.

The drawback of the system is that although the statistics can be downloaded and saved on the user's hard disk, they cannot be viewed while at the website. Hence you could download the wrong table and have to return to the site to look for an alternative – a potentially frustrating process.

The Treasury site has a sizeable quota of resources of relevance for investors, including details of ministerial speeches and a particularly interesting section which gives a detailed comparison of the forecasts made by 40 or so independent forecasters who publish analysis of the UK economy. This is divided into 'city' and 'non-city' forecasters and is produced by the Treasury on a monthly basis. This table in particular is an extremely useful guide to the broad expectations of leading so-called 'expert' forecasters.

Another useful facility is the ability to receive press releases direct from the Treasury as they are issued. You do this by subscribing to an e-mail list. Sadly this is 'read-only': investors are unable to reply with comments on Treasury policy! Many of the releases are mundane ones relating to the nuts and bolts of government policy and are not confined solely to material of direct interest to financial markets. Whether or not you subscribe to the list will depend on your level of interest in economic policy.

Another interesting feature of the site is a link to the Treasury's Euro business website (**www.euro.gov.uk**). This contains useful information on the introduction and impact of the Euro.

The Bank of England (**www.bankofengland.co.uk**) offers some interesting information relevant to investors. Available at the site are details of the minutes of the bank's monetary policy committee, the body responsible for setting interest rates in the UK. There are also details of speeches by bank officials and various working papers and other documents and statistics. It is a well-designed site and easy to navigate.

EU

The EU has its own statistical products that overlay those produced by member states' statistical offices. They are disseminated by Eurostat, which is accessed via a link from the EU's Europa site (**www.europa.eu.int**). It is responsible for collecting statistics across Europe.

The site offers a number of statistics and a forward calendar of releases. It is necessary to register to access certain parts of the site but the areas most relevant for investors are free. There is also an e-mail alert service for news releases.

Although the site looks needlessly complicated, due to its somewhat heavy design, it does have a good sitemap and is easy to use.

The European Central Bank (**www.ecb.int**) includes a link to the official Euro site (**www.euro.ecb.int**), press releases (including a regular monthly bulletin) and speeches by the president and executive board members. Various statistics can be downloaded from the site but the explanation regarding this process seems unduly complicated. Some independent observers have, however, ranked the site as one of the best among those of leading central banks.

US

From the standpoint of easy availability of free and timely releases of important data to financial markets and investors, the US stands head and shoulders above the rest. Having said that, there is a proliferation of statistical organizations within the US. This makes accessing the appropriate one something of a chore. There are some shortcuts you can use.

> From the standpoint of easy availability of free and timely releases of important data to financial markets and investors, the US stands head and shoulders above the rest.

The Economic Statistics Briefing Room site (**www.whitehouse.gov/fsbr/esbr**) has links to the full range of federal economic indicators, information on the timing of future announcements and a huge variety of supporting information. For information on the GDP, the Bureau of Economic Analysis (**www.bea.doc.gov**) provides all the relevant information with detailed tables. This site also provides access to research papers and analytical presentations by BEA staff.

Fedstats (**www.fedstats.gov**) has links to over 100 US federal agencies. These are listed alphabetically at the Fedstats site, together with the information they provide. The site also has a subject-based index. Fedstats aggregates the statistics available online from its various constituent agencies, as well as press releases from all the individual agencies, in a central, easily accessible system. This is known as Ferret (Federal Electronic Research, Review and Extraction Tool) and can be downloaded from the site.

This system provides access to data from the Bureau of Economic Analysis and allows you to select information interactively. You can, for example, make a selection from a scrollable list on a form. You can view the data in a variety of formats and print or download the spreadsheets.

The Federal Reserve occupies a key position in both the American and world economy, setting interest rates and monitoring monetary conditions in the US. It has its own news releases site (**www.federalreserve.gov**). This has a variety of information, including details of the chairman's public speeches and evidence to congressional committees.

STAT-USA (**www.stat-usa.gov**) has general data available by subscription only, as the taxpayer does not fund the service. The site does, however, have press releases and an online newsletter free of charge.

Several major international agencies are also based in the US. These include the World Bank, the IMF and several other development agencies. The most important from the standpoint of the production of economic statistics is the IMF.

The IMF's site contains some interesting fact sheets on the workings of the organization, including a question on everybody's lips: 'Where does the IMF get its money?' The site has press releases and downloadable statistics on a range of topics, both general and country-specific. The IMF has developed a code of good practice to encourage its members to create strong and uniform standards. The site has a list of countries that have subscribed to the IMF's special dissemination standard. These countries make a commitment to observe the standard and to provide information about their data and data dissemination practices.

Table 2.9 lists the useful UK, EU and North American sites.

Table 2.9 UK, EU and North American sites

Organization	URL	Graphics	Advance release dates	Search/ sitemap	Press releases	Key indicators	Publications	Free?	E-mail contact	Links?	Score
Bank of England	www.bankofengland.co.uk	Low	Yes	Yes	Yes	Yes	Yes	No	Yes	Yes	9
Eurostat	www.europa.eu.int	Medium	Yes	Yes	Yes	Yes	Yes	No	Yes	Yes	9
Office of National Statistics	www.statistics.gov.uk	Low	Yes	Yes	Yes	Yes	Yes	Yes	Yes	Yes	10
Treasury	www.hm-treasury.gov.uk	Low	No	Yes	Yes	Yes	Yes	Yes	Yes	Yes	9
European Central Bank	www.ecb.int	Low	Yes	Yes	Yes	Yes	Yes	Yes	Yes	Yes	10
Bureau of Economic Analysis	www.bea.doc.gov	Low	Yes	Yes	Yes	Yes	Yes	Yes	Yes	Yes	10
Economic Statistics Briefing Room	www.whitehouse.gov.fsbr	Low	No	Yes	Yes	Yes	Yes	Yes	Yes	Yes	9
Fedstats	www.fedstats.gov	Low	Yes	Yes	Yes	Yes	Yes	Yes	Yes	Yes	10
Federal Reserve	www.federalreserve.gov	Low	Yes	Yes	Yes	Yes	Yes	Yes	No	Yes	9
Statistics Canada	www.statcan.ca	Low	Yes	Yes	Yes	Yes	Yes	Yes	Yes	Yes	10

Source: author; www.linksitemoney.com

Timing of releases

Share and bond markets are obsessed by the here and now. So there is considerable focus on the monthly calendar of releases from the statistics organizations. This is particularly true of those in the US, UK, EU, Japan and other major countries.

Given the volume of separate statistical releases produced each month by each of these major countries, it is often the case that each stock market trading day will see significant announcements of economic statistics in one or other major market. As outlined above, many statistical organizations provide an advance calendar of the expected release dates of the most closely watched statistics to aid forecasters and commentators.

An easy way to keep tabs on this is to look at the financial press. Both *The Wall Street Journal Europe* and the *Financial Times* have a table in the paper each Monday showing the key market indicators being announced that week (along with results due from major companies).

One problem with this is that for a variety of reasons it does not seem possible for major announcements in different countries related to, say, inflation or money supply to be synchronized. Hence, in the week I am writing this, for example, the UK is announcing inflation data, unemployment, money supply and retail sales, the US is releasing industrial production, housing starts and a variety of other figures, Germany is announcing wholesale prices and so on.

However, Euro-zone countries do appear to be moving their announcements closer together. In the week in question, the 'EU-12', France and Italy are all announcing industrial production figures.

What to watch for is a moot point. Financial markets are often not entirely logical in the attention they pay to economic statistics and other key market indicators. I have already mentioned that they sometimes concentrate on the less accurate but quickly produced headline numbers, ignoring subsequent revisions. Moreover the markets sometimes focus unduly on different statistics at different times, depending on the prevailing market mood and investor psychology.

It is, however, fair to say that among the most closely watched figures in the US and Europe are money supply, inflation, gross national product (GNP) growth, unemployment, consumer confidence and industrial confidence. All of these and more will be covered in detail in later chapters. The next chapter deals with forecasters, how they work, and the data and information they provide that investors can use.

IN BRIEF

- The quality of statistical information varies considerably from country to country, sometimes making it difficult to find the relevant information.

- Most statistical organizations are government agencies. The quality of their research depends on the number of people employed relative to the amount of statistical information produced.

- Apart from individual countries, groups such as OPEC, the EU and OECD also provide information.

- Non-governmental groups, such as trade associations, also compile information but their self-interest does not always reflect the true picture.

- Statistical information and commentary is widely available in print form and at websites.

- The content and design of websites is not uniform and varies considerably from country to country.

- The US has a proliferation of statistical organizations but these can be narrowed down to those considered the most useful for an investor.

- The monthly release calendar is of special importance to the time-sensitive bond and stock markets. Unfortunately major announcements from different countries are not synchronized.

Who forecasts them?

There is an old saying. However many economists you lay end to end, you will never reach a conclusion. A politician, exasperated by the equivocation for which Treasury economists are known, was once also heard to call for a 'one-handed economist' so that he would not say 'on the other hand'.

Economists get bad press. Nigel Lawson, when he was Chancellor, delivered the famous put-down that they were 'teenage scribblers'. The scribblers later went out of their way to point out when Lawson's own forecasts were inaccurate – even though, as it turned out, theirs had been no better.

Economic forecasting has been practised for quite some time in various forms. Japanese traders used arcane chart patterns to forecast the prices of rice as far back as the 17th century. More recently the development of computing power has allowed researchers to crunch huge volumes of data in various permutations. They do this to see whether any meaningful economic relationships can be discerned. The result is that economic forecasting has become an industry.

Sometimes, though, it seems as though computing power has replaced thought, logic and an understanding of the human condition. In many spheres economics has become a branch of mathematics.

So who precisely are the forecasters, what do they forecast, how do they work and how accurate are they?

Adam Smith's army

On most economists' bookshelves (my own included) you will find a copy of a two-volume book, *An Enquiry into the Nature and Causes of the Wealth of Nations*, written by the 18th-century economist Adam Smith. Alongside it, and depending on when you received your training in the black arts of economics, you might find books by John Maynard Keynes, Milton Friedman and even Karl Marx.

Smith has long since been buried in an unpretentious grave in a small churchyard in one of the older parts of Edinburgh. He saw himself not as an economist but as a student of human nature. It shows you how far economic forecasting has come. Now what matters more is an ability to manipulate numbers and algebra rather than to discern the impulses that guide human actions.

According to William Sherden's excellent book *The Fortune Sellers* (John Wiley, 1998), there are close to 150,000 economists in the US. On a *prorata* basis, that would suggest perhaps 40,000 in the UK. As Sherden points out, they are all, in one form or another, in the business of either making or interpreting predictions.

A range of organizations employs economic forecasters. They include government finance ministries, central banks, large companies, banks, investment firms, universities, trade associations, and international bodies like the IMF and OECD.

Some economic forecasts are secret. Companies employ forecasters in specific areas that may be relevant to their businesses. This can include forecasting currencies that may affect the profits of their businesses overseas, or predicting the prices of the raw materials they use. On the other hand, many economic forecasts either attract or seek publicity. Academics publish forecasts for the reason that most academics publish anything – to prove their erudition.

Academics publish forecasts for the reason that most academics publish anything – to prove their erudition.

Banks and investment houses, however, see economic forecasting as a competitive weapon. Good accurate economic forecasts supposedly add lustre to the firm. It means that the company analysts they employ will be better informed and should attract business away from competitors.

Fund managers contribute forecasts to the City consensus, presumably as a way of suggesting to potential clients or investors that they have their heads screwed on. They also need to show that they are not just taking the forecasts provided by investment banks as the gospel truth.

International organizations produce forecasts because … well, perhaps because they don't want to feel left out.

In addition to these high-profile bodies there are significant numbers of independent economic forecasters and consultants. Some of them, with fewer axes to grind or vested interests to satisfy, may do a better job of forecasting than their larger peers.

The point about many of these forecasters is not that there are so many of them but that so few of the forecasts are accurate. Another gibe aimed at economists is that they have forecast nine of the last five recessions. In fact this criticism is now out of date, since many economists steadfastly refused to forecast the recent economic downturn or the previous four such periods, even when the evidence of it was becoming very clear indeed. Indeed, during these periods, most forecasters were predicting robust increases in economic activity.

That is one reason why I decided to write this book – to explain how market indicators and economic statistics work so you can make your own judgements.

Sherden's book says: 'Economic forecasters have routinely failed to foresee turning points in the economy: the coming of severe recessions, the start of recoveries, and periods of rapid increases or decreases in inflation.'

S I D E B A R

Scribblers in the stocks, The Times, 1998. One forecaster's view of his peers

Tim Congdon, a former economist at a City firm turned independent consultant, is scathing about the quality of City forecasting.

Pointing to the close (but ultimately incorrect) consensus pitted against Nigel Lawson's own forecasts in the late 1980s, he observed: 'All nine forecasts were closely bunched together and were therefore all equally inaccurate … Indeed, the gap between the City consensus and the likely outturn is far greater than the gap between the nine separate forecasts.

'A cynic new to the forecasting game, unaware of the great skill and care with which City analysts carry out their work, their undoubted intellectual courage and the enormous salaries which reward their efforts, might conclude that they are much better at copying each other than at predicting the future course of the economy.'

There is an explanation for this, apart from a predilection of City folk to avoid risking their careers and fat pay packets by moving too far away from a cosy consensus. It is that all the forecasters use similar thinking and similar computerized forecasting models, producing the same flawed results every time.

How do the forecasters work?

Despite all the computing power that goes into it, forecasting economic data still remains more art than science. The only way forecasters can work is from the past. They take the past data on the economy and attempt to work out the relationships between different parts of it. They move from that to attempting to judge at what stage in the business cycle we are currently at. Then they suggest a forecast on the basis of what has happened in previous similar cycles.

It is probably right to be sceptical about any wholly quantitative approach to analyzing the UK economy – and any attempt to forecast its key components. It may be possible to correlate one economic variable with another for example, but as every statistician is taught on his mother's knee, this does not prove there is any cause and effect in the relationship.

The Ernst & Young ITEM Club uses the Treasury Economic Model as its forecasting starting point. In 2000 it produced forecasts that accorded with those of the Treasury but were some way away from the actual outturn. In order words, the ITEM Club is adept at forecasting what the Treasury is forecasting, but not the economy itself.

Economic forecasting, whether computerized or not, is only as good as the data that it uses and the validity of the assumptions it makes. The shifting nature of economic relationships, the change in importance of different sectors of the economy, and the importance of human behaviour in the whole scheme of things makes formulating these assumptions difficult.

There is one simple example of this. This is the behaviour of the consumer in the US in the immediate aftermath of stock market falls in 2000 and 2001. Having borrowed heavily to finance excessive consumption as interest rates were falling, whether or not the consumer would be encouraged to continue spending and so bolster economic activity assumed major importance. Since such an extended spending boom was without precedent in the US (with the possible exception of during the late 1920s), it was hard to judge whether or not, in the fevered climate, the boom would continue or whether, as seemed more likely, economic uncertainty and job losses would lead Americans to cut back on consumption and begin saving again.

It goes to show only one thing. Predicting the behaviour of the consumer is about as susceptible to rational statistical analysis as predicting the future course of the stock market.

One other problem is the importance that is given to prevailing fashions in economic thought. In his book *Reflections on Monetarism*, Tim Congdon alludes to the inaccuracy of the Treasury Model in the 1970s. The inaccuracy arose because of the reluctance of its developers to accord sufficient importance to the inclusion of monetary aggregates, a decision made simply because studying money supply was not the fashion of the time.

In the end one can only judge by results. So in a sense the question to ask is not how the forecasters do it, but whether or not their forecasts are accurate.

Are their forecasts accurate?

In *The Fortune Sellers*, William Sherden reviewed 16 years and more of economic forecasting. It was an attempt to get a perspective on whether or not economic forecasters were accurate or not.

He came to the conclusion that they were not.

The argument has several strands. In the first place, Sherden argues, most economists over this period were no good at predicting turning points in the economy. Sherden takes the forecasters to task for seeking spurious precision in numbers and paying less attention to getting the big picture right.

This fault is blatantly apparent today in certain sections of the news media. Here slavish adherence to the latest 'number' appears to be the be-all and end-all. Questioning the validity of such an approach is to risk being branded a pedant or a killjoy.

Second, Sherden suggests that the further out the forecasts are being made, the less accurate they are likely to be. Intuition suggests this is true. Errors in predicting GDP growth rates, he claims, are as high as 45%, even at the start of the year being forecast. The error rate rises to 60% if one makes the starting point six months earlier. As Sherden puts it: 'Economists' forecasting skill on average is about as good as guessing.'

It is often the case, he says, that the best forecast in any year will be 'no change on the figure for the previous year'. No change is more likely to be right than the figure arrived at by sophisticated econometric analysis and hours of computing time by highly paid forecasters.

The book also claims that there are no forecasters who emerge consistently ahead of the pack, either in general terms or in predicting any particular economic statistic. Nor it seems do sophisticated computer models produce any better results. An instinctive guess with a backward glance to what happened last year is worth as much as a model with hundreds of equations.

Somehow it's encouraging to the amateur investor. He or she stands as good a chance as a professional economist as coming to the correct judgement of the significance or otherwise of a particular statistic.

Nor, claims Sherden, is there much comfort to be gained in looking at consensus forecasts. They may average out some of the wilder or more biased forecasts. But they are no more likely to predict economic turning points than the individual forecasts that make them up. There is also, he says, little evidence to suggest that forecasting accuracy is improving over time.

The obvious point is a simple one. The reason is that even complex mathematical models cannot reproduce the staggering complexity of the real economy. The real economy simply has too many complicated connections, logical and illogical, rational and irrational, calculated and emotive, economic and behavioural.

One quote from Sherden's book is bound to strike a chord with many investors, perplexed at the way events unfold. Likening the economy to the scientific construct of a complex system, he says: 'Complex systems exhibit periods of order and predictability, punctuated by unexpected moments of self-generated turmoil, which is why economists cannot predict the turning points in the economy.' He adds that complex systems adapt to their environments and change their behaviour accordingly, and have no fixed cycles.

What conclusions should one draw from this rather bleak view of economic forecasting? The first is that a broad approach to interpreting the numbers as they are reported is probably best. There is not much to be gained from reacting instantly to numbers that may or may not have significance. One need not react simply because they are better or worse than some bogus consensus. They may in any case be revised significantly at some later date.

It is better that we know in broad terms what the numbers signify. Then we can make the judgements for ourselves rather than be influenced by the forecasters. Is the economy expanding or contracting? Are the numbers themselves really that significant? Do they confirm the trends set by other statistics?

At the end of 2000 (and indeed every year), newspapers compared the forecasts made by leading investment bank economists and other prominent forecasters with the actual outturn. They gave the forecasters marks out of ten for their closeness or otherwise to the actual outturn (see Table 3.1).

Table 3.1 Which forecasters did best in 2000

	Score		Score
HSBC	10	Business Strategies	8
Warburg Dillon Read	10	Primark	8
Barclays Bank	10	DrKW	8
Credit Lyonnais	10	Merrill Lynch	8
CBI	10	NIESR	8
DRI	9	Williams de Broe	8
EIU	9	Barclays Capital	8
Greenwich Natwest	9	Cambridge Econometrics	8
Goldman Sachs	9	ABN Amro	8
Henley Centre	9	Deutsche Bank	8
Lombard Street	9	EC	7
CSFB	9	Société Générale	7

Note: Scores calculated on the basis of accuracy of forecasts of GDP growth, inflation, current account balance, unemployment rate and end-of-year base rate.

Source: Financial Times

One of the more amusing aspects of this exercise in 2000 was that the Treasury team got only 6 out of 10 for forecasting the British economy. This was despite the fact that, in theory it least, it should have had the best data and the best model. One of the interesting features was that UK and European-based investment banks appeared to be the best forecasters, whereas US-based ones did not (with the possible exception of Goldman Sachs). Organizations like the CBI, the Economist Intelligence Unit (EIU) and the Henley Centre, for example, proved better forecasters than organizations like JP Morgan, Daiwa, Schroder Salomon Smith Barney, the OECD and the Treasury itself.

Table 3.2 shows the average of the 2002 forecasts being made for some of the key economic variables, together with the average for the new forecasts and the range.

What is quite apparent is that there is a huge range among the forecasts for some of the variables. The gulf is so wide as to render the notion of a 'consensus' produced by the average meaningless. At the very least this should give pause for reflection that the methods that produce such a disparity of opinion cannot all be equally rigorous or indeed all be using the same data in the same way.

To sum up then, the problems with forecasters include:

- too much spurious precision

- forecasts less accurate the further out they're made

- 'no change' often the best forecast

- no forecasters consistently accurate

- sophistication of forecasting no guide to accuracy

- consensus is invariably wrong

- forecasting not improving over time.

Table 3.2 Consensus forecasts for UK economy in 2002

Item	Dec 01 forecast average	Lowest	Highest	Average of new forecasts
GDP growth (%)	1.8	0.4	2.6	1.9
Q4 RPI (%)	2.3	1.5	4.1	2.3
Q4 RPIX (%)	2.2	1.5	3.3	2.1
Q4 unemployment (m)	1.09	0.91	1.33	1.09
Current account (£bn)	−24.1	−35.2	−18.0	−24.3
PSNB for 2002/03 (£bn)	6.9	−3.5	15.0	8.3

Source: HM Treasury

Information on economic forecasts

Print media

Most of the heavyweight financial press does a good job of communicating information when data on major market indicators is to be published. How the number that comes to be accepted as the consensus is discovered is more of a mystery.

Journalists being what they are, they may pay more attention to the forecasts of high-profile commentators, with little effort made to distinguish expert from non-expert. However, magazines such as *The Economist* and US business publications like *Fortune* and *Business Week* usually display information about economic data impartially. *The Economist* is particularly good in this respect.

General articles on economics and forecasting

For more general background information and reading on economics, there is a range of sites from high-profile economists and market strategists. While they do not necessarily play the forecasting game, many have a common-sense view of events as well as vast experience.

Peter Bernstein, author of *Against the Gods* (Wiley, 1996) (an excellent book about the nature of risk), has a website at **www.peterlbernsteininc.com**, which has a selection of his articles on economics and portfolio strategy.

Samuel Brittan (**www.samuelbrittan.co.uk**) is an economics commentator for the *Financial Times*. Some of the articles on the site deal with his views on economic forecasting, which he describes as being part of the entertainment industry.

Academic economists can be dour. But some are excellent communicators, with a good sense of how to present ideas in a way the man in the street can understand. A site at **http://web.mit.edu/krugman/www/** has articles and contributions by Paul Krugman, while Robert Schiller, the Yale economist and author of 'Irrational Exuberance' (Princeton, 2000), a text on the 'bubble' of 2000, has a site at **www.econ.yale.edu/~schiller/**. Wharton school economists have their own site at **http://knowledge.wharton.upenn.edu**.

General information websites

There are several general sites related to economics and economic statistics. One of the best on offer is from Ed Yardeni, (**www.yardeni.com**) formerly chief investment strategist at Deutsche Banc Alex Brown in New York. The site has a comprehensive selection of research and statistics and can be accessed in eight languages. There are several pages of economic charts with the latest key indicators from round the world. The US section includes audio briefings, tables and news releases.

The site also has an extensive selection of links to statistics organizations, economics research, think-tanks, central banks and other organizations plus newspapers, online research services and other sources of information. One of the most entertaining links is to the 'Dead Economists Society', dedicated to 'the appreciation of the extraordinary insights of classical liberal economics'.

The Dismal Scientist (**www.dismal.com**) takes its name from the nickname for economics as first coined by the philosopher and historian Thomas Carlyle. Carlyle referred to economists as 'respectable professors of the dismal science', a name that has stuck. This site is quite simply one of the clearest on the web when it comes to identifying the timing of announcements and consensus expectations for major economic statistics. It is a leading provider of economic analysis, without being overladen with jargon. Much of the content is aimed at US users but other major world markets are covered. There is also a good page of classified links related to economics and statistics.

Also worthy of note is Intermoney (**www.intermoney.com**), operated by the economics consultancy IDEAGlobal. This contains crisply written comments on economics and bond and foreign exchange markets. In contrast to the situation a couple of years or so ago, much of the site's content is now password protected and for subscribers only.

Forecasters' websites

As noted elsewhere in this book, economic forecasts are not in short supply. Professional forecasters range from economists at investment banks to university professors, consultants and chief economists at leading companies, plus those at trade associations and other interested bodies.

The Treasury lists those economic forecasters that submit forecasts to it. It collects the forecasts to enable it to compile a table that gives the general consensus figures for a wide range of variables. The Treasury itself also makes forecasts. Many of the professional forecasters on the Treasury list make some or all of their data available to the outside world either in print form, on their websites, or both. In some instances research distribution is restricted to clients of the firm in question.

What follows was derived from an inspection of the sites of various economic forecasters conducted in late 2001. Sites may have changed since then, but the survey gives a brief flavour of what's on offer.

It's worth making the point that, unlike corporate websites, where lack of transparency often indicates lack of clarity, economic forecasters' websites may restrict access, but this is often purely a commercial consideration and does not indicate necessarily that the forecaster has anything to hide.

That said, good design is an ideal worth pursuing, yet many sites do not attain it. In the tables later in this section we have scored each of the forecaster's sites on the basis of their general design and accessibility qualities. We also rate them on whether they possess eight further attributes that make them useful from the standpoint of the man in the street trying to get to grips with economic forecasting. Generally, the more comprehensive the data available and the cleaner the design, the higher the score. Sites are rated out of a maximum possible 10.

When it comes to ease of navigation, low-intensity graphics get 2 points, medium 1 point and heavy, hard-to-navigate sites 0. Sites were rated on eight other attributes:

■ whether the site is searchable

■ whether it provides a site map

■ whether the site is exclusively devoted to economic research or has a specific section devoted to it

■ whether there is a clear statement of current economic forecasts

■ whether there is an explanation of the methods used to arrive at the forecasts

■ whether a reasonable amount of research is available free of charge

■ whether publications can be ordered online

■ whether it is possible to e-mail an economist at the firm to pose a query.

I think forecasters' sites should have:

■ good navigation

■ a sitemap

■ search facilities

■ a specific part devoted to economic research

■ clear statement of forecasts

■ explanation of forecasting methods

■ free research online

■ the facility to order publications online

■ the facility to e-mail a query.

Forecasters are split between commercial organizations in the City – including investment banks and consultancies – and other firms. The distinction between the two is sometimes hard to define. The next few paragraphs cover the websites of commercial entities.

Appraisal of City forecasters' sites

ABN Amro (**www.abnamro.com**) is a Dutch investment bank with a significant presence in the UK. It has a section of its site devoted to economic
research. Its 'Euroland Economics Update' is delivered weekly by e-mail free
of charge once you have registered.

This report contains key figures, macroeconomic and financial forecasts and the
latest key statistics. For more information on a regular basis you need to subscribe
to 'Economic Perspectives'. This is a monthly publication covering areas such as the
global economic outlook, special topics such as oil price developments, and a
broad range of economic data including macroeconomic forecasts. A year's subscription costs $106, although abstracts are available online free of charge.

Merrill Lynch's site (**www.ml.com**) is a mine of information. The flagship
publication of the Global Economics Department is a weekly economic and
financial commentary on the indicators for the current week. There is special
emphasis on the figures on the economy, corporate earnings and interest rates.

Another weekly online publication is an overview given by the Economics,
Investment Strategy, Market Analysis, and Fixed-Income and Quantitative
Analysis departments. Recent research reports are online. These include
'Global Research Highlights', a regular look at global markets.

Barclays Bank (**www.barclays.com**) does not have a site devoted purely to
economic research. The information can be found in various sections of its
corporate site, such as the bank's 'Economic Review'. This is a quarterly publication which assesses economic and financial developments in the UK and
internationally and includes key forecasts. The bank also publishes a commodities survey twice a year and makes forecasts for all industry sectors.
Economic data is in the corporate banking section of the site. This section
gives access to economic reports covering more than 40 countries and a
wide range of businesses and industrial sectors.

Capital Economics (**www.capitaleconomics.com**) is an independent consultancy based in London and run by Jonathan Loynes and Roger Bootle, a
well-known City economist. The two formerly produced the 'Greenwell Gilt
Weekly', a widely read research publication on the UK government bond
market. Bootle has also written books and has been a regular guest on financial news programmes. Capital Economics specializes in macro-economic
analysis. Research is available only to clients, although some samples are
available to registered users.

Lombard Street Research is an independent economic consultancy firm. Its
web presence, at **www.lombard-st.co.uk**, is primarily a subscription-only site.
Some free research can be obtained once you register as a user. Unlike some
other sites this is a straightforward process and gives immediate access. There

is a daily online news section. Lombard's analysts provide additional insights into current economic trends.

Professor Tim Congdon, the founder of Lombard Street Research, writes the monthly review, which analyzes UK economic affairs (six months of recent issues are on the site). A well-known economist and expert on monetary policy, Congdon's views on economic forecasting and its shortcomings are aired elsewhere in this chapter.

Other research from Lombard Street, such as its current 'Quarterly UK Economic Forecast', is available to clients only. Some previous issues are included on the site as an example of the company's research.

The Daiwa Institute of Research (**www.dir.co.jp**) describes itself as a 'comprehensive think-tank'. Linked to the Japanese securities house, it provides services in a variety of fields, including macro- and microeconomic research and reports on new technology. There are a number of free economic and strategy reports online. These include the firm's monthly economic review and a quarterly economic outlook.

Research information from Citigroup is at the site of its investment banking subsidiary Schroder Salomon Smith Barney (**www.salomonsmithbarney.com**). Most of the information at this site is available only to clients, but there is a free market update containing the latest perspectives on current events. In similar vein, an economic update is available.

Credit Suisse First Boston (**www.csfb.com**) currently offers access to its research only to institutional and corporate clients, although you can buy research reports by e-mailing CSFB and stipulating your area of interest. There are numerous press releases on the site, some of which give an inkling as to the firm's views on various economic issues. The firm publishes a comprehensive annual survey that looks at long-term relationships between bonds and equities. (Barclays Capital publishes a similar guide.).

Deutsche Bank Research (**www.dbresearch.com**) offers free research on its site. It focuses on the identification and analysis of economic, social and political trends and their potential effects on the economy. The research is in the form of publications, speeches and presentations. There is a link to Dr Ed Yardeni's site. Yardeni (see above) is the firm's chief investment strategist and is based in New York. Also on the site is a brief daily commentary, 'Talking Point'. This looks at economic and market trends.

Morgan Stanley (**www.morganstanley.com**) has economists located in five major financial centres round the world. They focus on themed macroeconomic research. The team publishes a wide range of printed and electronic products. This is, however, available only to clients. However, the website does feature a daily worldwide 'economic viewpoint'. It also has a weekly commentary from Morgan Stanley's chief economist, which is available as a webcast.

Though many investment funds are on the Treasury's list of forecasters, in many cases their research is purely for internal consumption. It therefore does not appear on their website. Royal & Sun Alliance Investments (**www.rsa-investments.com**) is an example of this. It has only a small amount of information on its site – brief economic forecasts and its global market view.

HSBC (**www.markets.hsbc.com**) has won various awards for its research, including a *Sunday Times* award for most accurate forecasting. In this it scored best out of a long list of forecasters, with rankings based on its accuracy at predicting five key economic variables. The 'global market comments' on the site deal mainly with interest rates. These cover numerous markets and are pretty up to date. For more detailed and varied research, however, it is necessary to register. Registration is a tedious process and can be accomplished only if the user can obtain an HSBC contact. In effect this restricts access to the firm's investment banking clients.

UBS Warburg (**www.ubswarburg.com**) is one step ahead of the other sites by offering a daily audio broadcast at 7.10 a.m. every morning dealing with global economic issues. Fortunately the recording of this is available throughout the day. Most of the research is only for clients but the site does include a monthly letter from the firm's chief economist.

WestLB Panmure (**www.westlb.com**) provides free economic research via the site of its German parent company. WestLB's economists offer forecasts on various global economies, as well as commenting on the outlook for major interest rates and currencies. Up-to-date weekly commentary and forecasts for the data of the coming week are also on the site.

Further information on the global economic development and detailed forecasts for the financial markets can be obtained from online publications. These include 'Economic Trends'. This is published monthly and covers the current economic situation in Germany and the Euro area. Also published monthly is an analysis of the developments on foreign exchange markets as well as short- and medium-term forecasts for the major currencies.

At the beginning of every quarter WestLB's 'International Financial Outlook' is published. This contains in-depth analyses and forecasts on the economy, inflation and interest and exchange rates for the major industrialized EU countries.

Standard Chartered (**www.standard-chartered.com**) specializes in research concerning Africa, Asia and Latin America, as befits its banking concentration in these areas. There are numerous free, detailed reports on the site as well as archive material. The reports include updates and outlooks on the economy of the regions covered.

There are various other City firms offering research on the web only to their clients. These include Barclays Capital (**www.barcap.com**), Dresdner Kleinwort Wasserstein (**www.drkw.com**), Goldman Sachs (**ww.gs.com**), Société Générale

Table 3.3 City forecasters' websites

Company	URL	Naviga-tion	Search-able	Site-map	Specific site or sub-site on econ. research	Clear state-ment of current forecasts	Explanation of fore-casting methods	Free economic research	Order print publica-tions online	E-mail a query	Score
ABN Amro	**www.abnamro.com**	Medium	Yes	Yes	Yes	Yes	No	Yes	No	Yes	7
Barclays Bank	**www.barclays.com**	Medium	No	Yes	No	Yes	No	Yes	No	Yes	5
Barclays Capital	**www.barcap.com**	Low	Yes	Yes	No	No	No	No	No	No	4
Capital Economics	**www.capitalecoNomics.com**	Low	No	No	Yes	No	No	No	No	No	4
Citigroup	**www.salomonsmithbarney.com**	Low	No	Yes	Yes	No	No	No	No	No	4
Credit Suisse First Boston	**www.csfb.com**	Low	Yes	Yes	No	No	No	No	Yes	Yes	6
Daiwa Institute of Research	**www.dir.co.jp**	Low	No	No	Yes	No	Yes	Yes	No	No	5
Deutsche Bank	**www.dbresearch.com**	Low	Yes	Yes	Yes	Yes	No	Yes	Yes	Yes	9
Dresdner Kleinwort	**www.drkw.com**	Low	Yes	Yes	No	No	No	No	No	Yes	5
Fortis Bank	**www.fortisbank.com**	Medium	Yes	Yes	No	No	No	No	No	Yes	4
Goldman Sachs	**www.gs.com**	Medium	Yes	Yes	No	No	No	No	No	No	3
HSBC Econ & Strategy	**www.markets.hsbc.com**	Medium	Yes	No	Yes	Yes	No	No	Yes	No	4
JP Morgan	**www.jpmorgan.com**	Low	Yes	Yes	No	No	No	No	No	No	4
Lehman Brothers	**www.lehman.com**	Low	Yes	Yes	No	No	No	No	No	Yes	5

Source: author; www.linksitemoney.com

Table 3.3 Continued

Company	URL	Navigation	Searchable	Site-map	Specific site or sub-site on econ. research	Clear statement of current forecasts	Explanation of forecasting methods	Free economic research	Order print publications online	E-mail a query	Score
Lombard Street	www.lombard-st.co.uk	Low	No	No	Yes	No	No	No	Yes	Yes	5
Merrill Lynch	www.ml.co.uk	Low	Yes	Yes	Yes	Yes	No	Yes	No	Yes	8
Morgan Stanley Dean Witter	www.morganstanley.com	Low	No	Yes	No	No	No	Yes	No	Yes	5
RBSFM	www.rbsmarkets.com	Low	Yes	No	No	No	No	No	No	No	3
Schroders	www.schroders.com	Medium	Yes	No	No	No	No	No	No	No	2
Royal & Sun alliance	www.rsa-investments.com	Medium	Yes	Yes	No	No	No	No	No	Yes	4
Société Générale	www.socgen.com	Medium	No	Yes	No	No	No	No	No	Yes	3
Standard Chartered	www.standard-chartered.com	Low	Yes	No	Yes	Yes	No	Yes	No	Yes	7
UBS Warburg	www.ubswarburg.com	Low	Yes	Yes	No	No	No	No	No	Yes	5
West LB Panmure	www.westlb.de	Low	Yes	No	Yes	Yes	No	Yes	No	Yes	7

(**www.socgen.com**), Lehman Brothers (**www.lehman.com**) and JP Morgan (**www.jpmorgan.com**). The latter does have some free information.

Table 3.3 summarizes the characteristics of these City forecasters' websites and what they score under our rating system.

As the table shows, the sites from Merrill Lynch and Deutsche Bank score best, although neither scores a perfect 10. ABN Amro and WestLB also rank highly on the information they make available free of charge to the average man in the street. Where almost all sites fall short is in providing a clear exposition of the methods used to arrive at their forecasts.

Appraisal of non-City forecasters' sites

Sites of organizations that fall outside the City and banking arena, as classified by the Treasury list at any rate, include the following.

Cambridge Econometrics (**www.camecon.co.uk**) specializes in economic modelling and forecasting and aims at the UK business sector. Consequently the reports that can be ordered through the site are costly. Some abridged versions can be purchased at an average cost of £45, covering the UK and Europe. A good deal of information can be gleaned from the press release section that outlines the reports. It includes some charts and graphs.

The Centre for Economic and Business Research (**www.cebr.dk**) is an independent research organization based in Copenhagen. It conducts research on economic and social issues of importance for medium- to long-term growth in Denmark. It professes to make a substantial contribution to bridging the gap between economic theory and its applications. Much of the published work is in Danish, although the discussion papers are in English. An abstract of the English content is provided on the site together with the e-mail address of the author.

> Extensive free information is provided in the form of analyses and commentary on the effects of worldwide events on the global economy.

DRI-WEFA (**www.dri-wefa.com**), a subsidiary of Global Insights, was formed in 2001 by an amalgamation of Data Resources Incorporated and Wharton Econometric Forecasting Associates. Its headquarters are in the US with offices worldwide. It analyzes political and financial trends for all the major world economies. Extensive free information is provided in the form of analyses and commentary on the effects of worldwide events on the global economy. A number of lengthier special studies on current and future issues are also available free of charge. It is possible to order reports online as well as being able to register for occasional global teleconferences.

The Economist Intelligence Unit (**www.eiu.com**) is part of the company that publishes *The Economist*. The website content is subscription-only. EIU is a well-known and widely respected forecaster and produces everything from global macroeconomic forecasts to political and economic analysis for almost 200 individual countries. It draws on the expertise of over 500 analysts, editors and correspondents. At the time of writing a 14-day free trial offer was available online, although this was aimed primarily at companies. It is, however, possible to purchase articles from the online store and have them delivered on screen immediately. The prices typically range from $4–25 at the time of writing.

The ITEM Club (**www.ey.com**) is an independent economic forecasting group sponsored by Ernst & Young. It is the only forecasting group to use the same economic model as the Treasury uses for its policy analysis and Budget forecasts. ITEM stands for 'Independent Treasury Economic Model'. In theory, the ITEM club's use of the Treasury model means that it is in a position to test whether government claims and forecasts are credible. ITEM produces quarterly forecasts and special reports. These can all be downloaded from the site. Summaries of the reports are also available on the site. Printed copies can be obtained by phoning the organization.

In forecasting terms ITEM is a conundrum. Because it uses the Treasury model, its published forecasts tend to be close to the Treasury's and sometimes equally wrong. The value members get from the club is in being able to manipulate the model as they wish and experiment to see the economic results of different economic assumptions.

The National Institute of Economic and Social Research (**www.niesr.ac.uk**), based in London, is an independent educational charity and works in co-operation with universities and other academic bodies. Free economic research is provided in the form of discussion papers, which can be downloaded from the site. As the title of the institute would suggest, much of this information is not of a purely economic nature. It publishes a quarterly economic review that contains, among other things, a detailed forecast of both the UK and other major economies and a commentary on issues in the economics sphere. This is available on subscription only. It currently costs £95 but summaries are available on the site free of charge. Some of the institute's press releases may be of interest and these can be received automatically by e-mail or viewed at the site free of charge. Subscription services provided on a commercial basis include monthly GDP estimates. These aim to give businesses access to accurate forecasts for UK GDP prepared on a similar basis to the figures from National Statistics that are published quarterly.

Oxford Economic Forecasting (**www.oef.com**) provides independent forecasting and analysis for business economists and planners. There is no free information available on the site but it is possible to register for a month's free trial.

The OECD (**www.oecd.org**) is an international organization with 29 member countries. It is based in Paris. The site contains details of the OECD's 'Economic

Outlook' publication. This provides a twice-yearly assessment of economic trends, prospects and policies in OECD countries. It is subscription-only but there is a long abstract on the site, which provides enough to be a useful background guide.

According to the site, the OECD offers 'conditional projections rather than forecasts', a euphemistic approach to forecasting that will fool few users. Although the site is poorly designed and underpowered, and therefore very slow to respond when accessed on a standard dial-up connection, it does have some interesting features. One particularly good one is a lengthy glossary of concepts and abbreviations. Among the other content on the site, the 'OECD Observer' is also worthwhile. This provides concise, up-to-date analyses of crucial world issues. The OECD online bookshop has numerous publications, available in either print or electronic form. The site also provides abstracts of speeches and presentations by the economics department, if that's what excites you.

The European Commission (**www.europa.eu.int**) has improved over what was a notoriously cumbersome site to negotiate. The Commission does sponsor some useful research, producing short-term macroeconomic projections twice-yearly, in the spring and autumn. These are online. Print copies can be ordered if necessary. The focus is on the Euro area and the member states of the EU, with forecasts provided for the following two years. Eurostat statistics are easy for registered users to access.

The Confederation of British Industry is the main employers' organization in the UK. As its website (**www.cbi.org.uk**) explains, it is a non-profit-making organization funded by subscriptions. As such it offers no free in-depth research. However, its publications, guides and surveys can be purchased through the online bookshop and there are numerous press releases on the site that may sometimes be of interest. Economic bulletins can be downloaded free of charge.

Table 3.4 provides a summary of the features of the sites of these non-City-based organizations and their scores out of 10.

In general, these sites scored marginally less than the City forecasters and are more likely to charge for their work. Of the ones covered, the ITEM Club and NIESR score best. The EU site would also be on a par with these were it not for the generally cumbersome navigation of the Europa site. Cambridge Econometrics also has a creditable offering.

A number of other international organizations, including the IMF and the World Bank, provide some information on economic trends within their sphere of influence. Generally, though, these sites are not specifically concerned with leading world economies. The IMF has led a crusade to get national statistics organizations to provide their statistics on a consistent and rigorous basis, for which it deserves considerable credit.

Table 3.4 Non-City forecasters' websites

Company	URL	Naviga-tion	Search-able	Site-map	Specific site or sub-site on econ. research	Clear state-ment of current forecasts	Explanation of fore-casting methods	Free economic research	Order print publica-tions online	E-mail a query	Score
Cambridge Econometrics	www.camecon.com	Low	Yes	No	Yes	Yes	No	No	Yes	Yes	7
CBI	www.cbi.org.uk	Low	Yes	Yes	No	No	No	No	Yes	Yes	6
CEBR	www.cebr.dk	Low	No	No	No	No	No	No	No	Yes	3
DRI-WEFA	www.dri-wefa.com	Low	Yes	Yes	Yes	Yes	No	Yes	Yes	Yes	9
EIU	www.eiu.com	Low	No	No	Yes	No	No	No	Yes	Yes	5
TEM Club	www.ey.com	Low	Yes	Yes	No	Yes	No	Yes	No	Yes	8
NIESR	www.niesr.ac.uk	Low	No	No	Yes	Yes	Yes	Yes	Yes	Yes	8
OEF	www.oef.com	Low	No	No	Yes	No	No	Yes	No	No	3
OECD	www.oecd.org	High	Yes	No	Yes	Yes	No	Yes	Yes	Yes	6
European Commission	www.europa.eu.int	Medium	Yes	Yes	No	Yes	Yes	Yes	Yes	Yes	8

Source: author; www.linksitemoney.com

I N   B R I E F

■ A range of organizations employs economic forecasters for various purposes.

■ The accuracy of forecasts should not be taken for granted.

■ The real economy is so complex that no mathematical model can reproduce its relationship with 100% accuracy.

■ A broad approach to interpreting the numbers is desirable. Instant reaction is not to be recommended. Do not rely entirely on forecasts.

■ The various methods used in forecasting produce a disparity of opinion.

■ Websites provide much information but do not usually disclose their forecasting methods.

■ City forecasters provide more free information on the whole than non-City ones do.

Prices and money

This chapter covers the market indicators that tell us about movements in price levels and the influences over them.

One of the most important is consumer price inflation, as measured by the RPI and its variants. Wholesale prices are also important because they can provide an early warning of changes in retail prices. Money supply – how much cash and credit we have to draw on and spend – is also an important factor in the economy at large. It has a direct impact on price inflation and the overall level of economic activity.

Inflation

Definition

The RPI in the UK is the main way in which inflation is measured. Inflation is a term used by statisticians and economists to denote general increases in prices paid by consumers and businesses for goods they need. Table 4.1 summarizes RPI jargon.

Table 4.1 RPI jargon

What it's called	What it means
RPI	Retail price index (UK)
RPIX	RPI excluding mortgage interest
RPIY	RPI excluding mortgage interest and indirect taxes
ROSSI	RPI excluding all housing costs
CPI-W	Consumer price index for urban wage earners (US)
CPI-U	Consumer price index for all urban households (US)
HIPC	Harmonized Index of Consumer Prices (inter-EU)

Alternative names

In the US and in certain other markets the RPI is known as the consumer price index (CPI). Essentially it means the same thing – a broad measure of price inflation. However, over the years politicians and statisticians have decreed that a broad CPI cannot reflect all of the nuances that may need to be taken into account in setting economic policy. This has resulted in several other sub-indices being set up. They exclude some items that are either not applicable to the whole population or which might distort comparisons.

In the UK, for example, there is the RPIX. This is the standard RPI index excluding mortgage interest payments. The RPIX was devised in order to divorce the underlying rate of price inflation from changes in the general level of interest rates (and hence mortgage rates).

The UK's National Statistics calculates the so-called ROSSI index. This is a version of the retail price index that excludes rent, mortgage interest payments, council tax and depreciation costs on owner-occupied property.

In the US, there are two sub-versions of the CPI. One measures prices for goods consumed by urban wage earners and the other covers all urban consumers. In contrast to the UK, rural consumers are excluded from the index in the US.

Member countries of the EU, including the UK, also calculate what is known as the Harmonized Index of Consumer Prices (HICP) for their territory. This is done so that changes in price levels can be compared between countries on a common basis.

How it's calculated

The UK RPI is an average measure of changes from month to month in the prices of goods and services bought by households in the UK. By definition the index has to make an assumption about how the average household in the UK spends its money. Government statisticians take the data gathered each year on household spending patterns (published in the Family Expenditure Survey). They then use it to work out the relative importance of the different items that go to make up the RPI.

> **Affluent investment bankers' purchases of champagne, yachts and country houses do not distort the picture.**

The expenditure of certain higher-income households and those of pensioners solely dependent on state benefits is excluded. Affluent investment bankers' purchases of champagne, yachts and country houses do not distort the picture.

The index uses a large representative selection of more than 650 items and measures price movements in them in 147 areas throughout the country. Some 130,000 separate price quotations are used each month in order to work out the index.

The RPIX is calculated in the same way, but simply excludes mortgage interest payments. The RPIY is the RPI but excludes both mortgage interest payments and the effect of changes in indirect taxations such as VAT and excise duties.

The HICP is calculated rather differently. The method used is broadly the same, using a spending basket and collecting data from a broad range of regions. But the HICP is a geometric rather than a weighted arithmetic average. The HICP also excludes certain items that are included in the UK RPI and includes others that are not.

It mainly excludes costs relating to owner-occupied housing, since this is a substantial point of difference in spending patterns between EU member countries. It includes (which the RPI does not) airfares and university tuition and accommodation fees, and costs of accommodation in nursing and retirement homes. Another point of difference is that the RPI takes only spending by private households, excluding the extremes. The HICP takes all households, those in institutions, and spending by foreign visitors.

In the US, the pattern is more or less the same as for the UK RPI, except that the spending basket is updated less frequently, typically once every ten years. This means that the spending patterns on which the CPI is based can be anything up to 15 years old. Nor does it reflect the spending habits of the rural population.

Recent changes

In the UK the RPI and related consumer price indices for a particular month are published in the middle of the following month.

Table 4.2 shows changes in the UK in 2001 and 2002.

Interpretation

Interpreting the monthly movements in the RPI can be tricky. For one thing it is only an average. Almost by definition it will not be representative of the change in your cost of living in the period. This is because you and your family will almost certainly buy different things in different quantities to the average household.

The RPI can also be hostage in almost every month to a host of one-off factors – seasonal changes in the price of fruit and vegetables, excise duty changes, summer discounting by retailers, changes in interest rates. Differences in timing from one year to the next in these factors can affect comparisons.

Table 4.2 Changes in the UK RPI

		All items (RPI)		All items excluding mortgage interest payments (RPIX)		Harmonized index of consumer prices (HICP)	
		Index Jan 87 is 100	% change over 12 months	Index	% change over 12 months	Index (1996 is 100)	% change over 12 months
2001	September	174.6	1.7	172.8	2.3	107.6	1.3
	October	174.3	1.6	172.6	2.3	107.4	1.2
	November	173.6	0.9	172.2	1.8	107.2	0.8
	December	173.4	0.7	172.5	1.9	107.5	1.0
2002	January	173.3	1.3	172.4	2.6	107.1	1.6
	February	173.8	1.0	172.8	2.2	107.3	1.5
	March	174.5	1.3	173.5	2.3	107.7	1.5

Source: National Statistics

The plethora of different measures of inflation can be a nightmare for commentators and forecasters alike. Broadcasters and commentators tend to forecast and comment on different things. Forecasts are often couched in the change in one month, whereas the running annual rate of inflation means more to the man in the street. A recent press release from National Statistics, for example, quoted:

- all items RPI up 0.3% in month
- all items RPI annual rate of 1.7%
- RPIX annual rate 2.3%
- RPIY annual rate 2.8%
- tax and price index annual rate 0.3% in month
- all goods index up 0.5% in month
- all goods annual rate 0.5%
- all services index up 0.3% in month
- all services annual rate 3.9%.

Which of these figures represents the best way of measuring the inflation rate? You pays your money and takes your choice.

The headline figure alluded to by most forecasters is normally the monthly change in the top-line RPI. Forecasts submitted to the Treasury by outside forecasters actually take none of these figures. They predict the annual rate seen in the forthcoming quarter compared with the same period a year previously.

S I D E B A R

Pitfalls in inflation figures ...

Remember above all that you need to distinguish between falling inflation – a fall in the rate at which prices are rising – and deflation (prices that are actually falling in absolute terms). Though the rate of inflation may be dropping, say from 3% a year to 2%, this still means prices are rising. Deflation, a rare phenomenon in the West in the last century, means prices are falling year by year, a quite different thing.

... and what inflation is not

Inflation is not a true measure of the cost of living. This can vary considerably from country to country and reflects the local exchange rate, labour costs and other factors. These variations, sometimes used to determine pay packages for executives on foreign assignment, can be extreme.

Taking the US as 100, for example, in 1999 the cost of living index for Zimbabwe was 42 and India 41, whereas in Japan the cost of living was 164 and in Hong Kong 120. Japan's cost of living is the highest in the world despite the fact that it has one of the lowest inflation rates in the world.

Why is it important for you?

In the US, UK and much of western Europe, inflation, as measured by the CPI in its various guises, has been low for some time. This has made people forget how important low inflation is for the economic well-being of most of us. High inflation is a corrosive force, creating uncertainty and redistributing income to those with economic clout and away from the weak and vulnerable. Those with fixed incomes are particularly vulnerable to high inflation.

Inflation also erodes the value of debt, to the detriment of anyone who has lent money. Governments tend not to suffer. On the whole they are borrowers, not lenders. Excise duties are frequently linked more or less automatically to inflation. And, though tax allowances are also adjusted upwards, the tendency for people to earn higher nominal incomes usually offsets this and takes them into higher tax brackets.

The fortunate have incomes directly linked to inflation, some civil service pensions being the most obvious example. The government has tended to have a link established between the state pension and average earnings, rather than price inflation, to the consternation of pensioners' pressure groups. Interest payments and capital repayments of index-linked government debt are pegged to the RPI.

Although there is no formal link, interest rates tend to be higher when inflation is high. This is because lenders must be compensated for the uncertainty that inflation brings with it and the erosion of the real value of borrowers' obligations.

In general high inflation is bad because it contributes to individuals and companies making bogus decisions. The clear signals that are given by relative differences in prices in a time of low inflation are blurred when price increases are rapid. No one knows where prices will be a few months hence. No one knows where they stand.

Serious inflation contributes to shortages, queues and hoarding. It inevitably reduces the external value of a country's currency (think of the effect inflation had on the value of the mark in early 1920s Germany). It makes imported goods more expensive to buy and leads people to favour physical assets over paper money.

Because of this governments have long attempted to control things to produce relatively stable prices. In practice, consumer price indices exaggerate the effective inflation rate slightly because they assume a fixed pattern of spending and do not take account of the fact that people's spending patterns may themselves shift because of price changes. Nor do they take into account, for example, new products and changes in quality. Taken together, estimates from US economists suggest that these can account for an annual rate of inflation of between 0.8 and 1.6 percentage points.

The UK government's goal in 2001/2002 has lately been an inflation rate in the region of 2%. Officials try to adjust economic policy to keep to this target. They do this mainly by controlling the supply of money in the economy and by raising and lowering the cost of borrowing money (interest rates). The next section touches on money supply and monetary policy.

Finally, keep in mind that from a historical perspective periods of high inflation, or indeed any inflation, have not been the norm. In 1914, the general level of prices was little different to that of 350 years earlier, the intervening years having seen periods of both rapidly rising prices and rapidly falling ones.

Table 4.3 summarizes what to earn and what to own at times of inflation and deflation.

Money supply

Definition

Money is anything that people will accept as payment. But this doesn't mean just the physical manifestation of coins and banknotes. Bank deposits count too. So money supply statistics measure the value of notes and coins in circulation, as well as some bank deposits.

Table 4.3 What to earn and what to own

Deflation	Inflation
Fixed income	Wage or salary
Lend money at fixed rates	Borrow money at fixed rate
Cash, gold	Physical assets (e.g. property)
Fixed-rate bonds	Index-inked government bonds

Money supply is a key indicator for overall economic activity. If money supply increases, it allows more or bigger transactions to take place and so the economy will grow. If money supply contracts, the economy will grow more slowly and ultimately shrink.

Alternative names

Money supply can cause considerable confusion. This is because of the different ways different countries define it. There is a plethora of 'M numbers' to denote different types of money. These range from M0 (pronounced 'M nought') to M5. As the numbers rise, in general terms the definition used for what constitutes money gets broader. M0, mainly used in the UK, consists of notes and coins but also includes commercial banks' deposits at the Bank of England. M1 is used outside the UK and is notes and coins plus 'instant-access' bank deposits. (See Table 4.4 for a definition of M numbers.)

M0 and M1, whichever is used, are called 'narrow money'. 'Broad money' is denoted by M2, M3, M5 or (in the UK) M4.

The UK does not release figures for M2, M3 or M5. In other countries, definitions again vary as to what constitutes broad money. Some or all of the following may be added in to M1 to create different measures: savings deposits, bank deposits with notice periods, money market funds, certificates of deposits, collateralized loans used for bond trading, public and/or private sector bank deposits and short-term debt with up to two years to go before repayment.

Table 4.4 Defining M

Number	As used in	Includes
M0	UK	Cash
M1	US	Cash, private sector demand deposits, traveller's cheques
M1	Japan	US M1 plus public sector demand deposits
M2	US	US M1 plus time deposits, money market funds
M2	Japan	Cash plus public and private sector deposits
M2	Euro-zone	M1 plus time deposits, deposits maturing <2yrs
M3	US	US M2 plus large money funds, deposits, repos, Euro$
M3	Euro-zone	M2 plus large money funds, repos, debt <2yrs maturity
M3	Japan	M2 plus CDs
M4	UK	UK M0 plus £ deposits of UK non-bank private sector

all measures from M2 upwards count as 'broad' money

For the purposes of comparing growth rates in money supply internationally, figures are usually given just for narrow and broad money. Differences in definition are ignored as being insignificant when it comes to comparing rates of change in the figures.

How it's calculated

For the sake of simplicity, we'll look at the UK definitions of narrow money and broad money, namely, M0 and M4.

In the UK, as noted above, M0 is simply notes and coins in circulation plus the unused balances that commercial banks have with the Bank of England. These are included because they can be turned into cash to satisfy demand from customers.

M4 is M0 (i.e. cash in circulation) plus deposits held at British banks by the non-bank private sector. In other words it does not include public sector bank accounts, or bank deposits held by overseas institutions, or money deposited by one bank with another. It does include current accounts and deposits owned by the likes of you and me at banks or building societies and larger deposits held by companies other than banks.

The Bank of England produces a range of statistics on the growth in money supply. These include monthly figures for changes in M0, M4 and M4 lending. M4 lending is the other side of M4.

While to you and me a bank deposit and the cash in our pockets represents an asset, to a bank it is an obligation. Banks do not sit on the deposits we make. They use them to make loans to other customers, putting money in their bank accounts or the bank accounts of suppliers they buy goods from.

So apart from a small reserve kept in case we demand our money back, for every asset there is a liability, and for every deposit there is a loan. So M4, because it includes deposits, also produces corresponding lending activity.

M4 and M4 lending, being two sides of the same coin, are roughly the same size. Loans and deposits made outside the scope of this definition account for any differences. This could be a loan to or from the public sector or to or from overseas. The main statistics are published monthly.

Typically growth rates are given on a seasonally adjusted basis. The figures show growth for the month in question, an annualized figure given for a three-month period, and the growth rate over a 12-month period. International comparisons, sometimes given in the financial press and in publications like *The Economist*, generally show the year-on-year growth in narrow and broad money.

Recent changes

In the UK, monthly money supply information is generally published in the course of the first week of the following month. Table 4.5 shows some changes in 2001 and early 2002.

Interpretation

There has been a great deal of debate over precisely how narrow and broad money should be defined and which measure is the most appropriate tool for the government to use in its quest to regulate economic activity.

In the US, there is greater focus on narrow money. But narrow money is defined more liberally in America, and includes some bank deposits. In the UK, M0 is an interesting concept, but it appears to have little predictive power. Most agree that it would be absurd to use its fluctuations as some sort of indicator of economic well-being.

> How much cash we have in our pockets at any one time is, for most of us, not a true indicator of our overall wealth.

How much cash we have in our pockets at any one time is, for most of us, not a true indicator of our overall wealth. Marks & Spencer does not decide whether or not to build a new store on the basis of how much cash it has in its tills on a Friday night.

Movements in M4 (or its predecessor, known as sterling M3) have proved a better guide to future changes in other economic variables.

Table 4.5 UK money supply statistics

Percentage growth rate in seasonally adjusted data over:						
	MO			M4		
	1 month	3 months*	12 months	1 month	3 months*	12 months
2001 December	0.8	8.3	7.9	−0.3	1.7	5.7
2002 January	1.0	10.4	8.0	0.5	1.9	5.9
February	0.2	8.1	7.1	0.5	3.5	5.3
March	0.5	6.8	7.2	−0.2	3.8	5.7
* Annualized rate						

Source: Bank of England

S I D E B A R

The quantity theory of money

In themselves, changes in money supply are less important than is sometimes claimed. It is their knock-on effects that are important. The reason so much attention is paid to money supply statistics dates back to an economic theory that appears well founded in fact.

At its crudest the so-called 'quantity theory of money' is expressed by the formula $MV = PQ$. The theory suggests that the quantity of money and the speed or velocity with which it circulates in the economy is matched by changes in quantity of goods and services produced and/or the general level of prices.

Subscribe to this and economic policy becomes a question of manipulating money supply (M) to produce steady growth in GDP (i.e. in Q), but only limited inflation (not much growth in P).

V, the velocity with which money circulates, is, in classical economics, assumed to be constant. This assumption is difficult to square with reality. But it is generally thought that if the economy is kept on an even keel – with modest monetary growth, modest inflation and modest growth in output – changes in V will be small.

The significance of money supply figures as a predictive tool has another dimension. It is that they are entirely within the control of the central bank, which controls both the level of interest rates and the supply of credit. Interest rates, the price of borrowed money, are covered in a later chapter. Direct control over the supply of money and credit is exercised by the Bank of England through the way in which the banking system operates and the central bank's ability to buy in and issue (sell) money market instruments and government bonds.

The banking system functions by taking in deposits from customers and lending money on the back of them. Because most customers draw down their deposits infrequently, it can lend out most of what is deposited in the form of loans. These loans become new deposits, a proportion of which can be lent out, which in turn become new deposits, and so on.

This means that, depending on how much is kept in reserve, there is a multiplier effect on the amount of credit each deposit will create. If banks keep, say, 10% of their deposits in the form of reserves, credit will ultimately be created equivalent to ten times the amount of the original deposit. If banks are forced to keep 20% in reserve, the system will create credit only up to five times the original deposit.

The Bank of England dictates the minimum level of reserves that must be kept in the form of easily cashable assets to meet withdrawals of deposits. One way it can control these reserves is by buying government bonds from or issuing them to the banking sector. This either injects cash into the banking system or siphons it out, reducing the ability of the banks to create credit.

If it issues government bonds and these are bought by the banking sector for cash, this reduces the banking sector's reserves and hence reduces the supply of credit in the economy. Similarly, if the central bank wants to increase the supply of credit, it can buy bonds from the banking sector, thus increasing their reserves and allowing them to lend more. These routine adjustments to the supply of credit are known as 'open market operations'.

The central bank can also unilaterally change the percentage and composition of the assets it requires banks to keep in liquid form to meet withdrawals, but this happens infrequently.

Under normal circumstances, to keep the economy on an even keel, the central bank will want to see money supply growing at a rate which allows for a target rate of inflation and an underlying rate of growth in the economy, avoiding hyperinflation on the one hand and 'boom and bust' rates of growth on the other. Inflation is likely to flare up into a serious problem only if economic growth outstrips the economy's productive capabilities.

The statistics on money supply growth, particularly the broad money measures, give a clear indication as to where the authorities believe the economy is headed. If it is overheating, the central bank will attempt to engineer slow growth in money supply. If it fears recession, the authorities will let the banking system supply more credit.

Why is it important for you?

Money supply has important implications for us as both investors and individuals. If the government is tightening up the supply of credit, it makes life tougher for businesses. Loans and overdrafts may be called in or not extended, creditors may be more insistent that their bills are paid quicker, if only because they are facing pressure themselves. Looser credit, as indicated by faster expansion of money supply, makes borrowing easier and creditors more relaxed.

Money supply statistics can also give some clues as to the way in which the prices of financial assets might move. In times of crisis, such as the terrorist attacks in New York in September 2001 and the earlier collapse of the LTCM hedge fund in 1998, central banks preserve the integrity of the banking system, which might otherwise seize up, by supplying virtually unlimited liquidity and publicizing the fact.

What is required subsequently, however, is for the excess liquidity to be mopped up. This is rarely publicized, so one needs to watch the statistics to try to divine whether or not it is happening. If it is not, it is likely to lead to surging prices, particularly of financial assets such as shares. It is said, for example, that the failure of the US Federal Reserve to mop up the liquidity injected into the financial system in the wake of the LTCM collapse and the extra liquidity supplied to the system to counter the supposed millennium bug were such events. It was responsible for the stock market bubble that subsequently burst in March 2000. Excess money in the economy has to find an outlet.

This is not to say that central bankers do a bad job. Freedom from political influence has become the norm among central banks in the US, UK, Europe and elsewhere, as has the setting of clear and unambiguous policy goals. This has not eliminated fluctuations in economic activity, but has made it some-what easier to mitigate their adverse effects.

Producer prices

Definition

Producer price indices (PPIs) measure the changes in prices charged by businesses (metaphorically 'at the factory gate') for the goods they produce. They are an alternative measure of inflation because ultimately retailers and distributors will pass on these prices to their customers.

Alternative names

In the UK, PPIs are divided into two: output prices and input prices. Output prices are 'factory gate prices' charged to customers. Input prices represent the cost of materials and fuel that manufacturers themselves bear. In the US, the PPI is divided into three, covering finished goods, intermediate materials and components, and raw materials. The PPI for finished goods is typically the statistic that the media pays attention to.

Most countries have adopted the PPI convention. Some include agriculture as well as manufacturing in the sphere of producer prices. By definition services are not included.

Media reports often also refer to PPI numbers as wholesale prices, although this is not correct. The US in fact changed the name of the wholesale price index (as it was originally known) to the PPI in 1978 to remove any confusion.

Producer prices are prices direct from domestic manufacturers. Wholesale price indices measure prices for goods distributed in bulk and can also include prices of imports. They were first introduced to measure raw material prices.

How it's calculated

Like the RPI and its variants, the PPI is calculated from a basket weighted according to the relative importance of the industry concerned. The size of the weighting is based on the value of an industry's production and how big or small it is in the overall scheme of things. If the widget industry accounts for 5% of GDP, then any changes in the prices it charges its customers will have a 5% weighting in the PPI.

Data on prices is collected from surveys conducted by the appropriate statistics organization. The recipients of the survey are selected by means of a stratified random sample. The sample is updated periodically to reflect changes in industrial structure and technology. In the UK this is National Statistics. In the US, for example, the appropriate body is the Bureau of Labour Statistics.

Returns flow in continuously and the index is therefore effectively an average for the month, even though respondents to the survey are asked to pinpoint prices on a particular day.

The US and the UK share a broadly similar method of calculating these indices, and the distinctions between the PPI for finished goods and the CPI/RPI can be summarized as in Table 4.6.

Table 4.6 Retail prices versus factory gate prices

	PPI	RPI
Covers	Consumer goods, capital goods (no services)	Consumer goods and services (no capital goods)
Prices	Received by producers	Paid by consumers
Sales taxes	Excluded	Included
Excise taxes	Included/excluded	Included
Collected	Over course of month	Over course of month
Method	Mail-in survey	In-store survey
Seasonal adjustment	Rarely used	Commonly used

In the UK, PPI figures are produced both including and excluding excise duties. A series is also produced excluding industries where excise duties have an effect, particularly tobacco, oil and food and beverages.

Despite the fact that some statisticians regard seasonally adjusting producer prices as a bit of a mug's game, National Statistics does produce seasonally adjusted figures, although it gives more weight to those that aren't. The statistics show both the month-on-month percentage change in the index (that is, September change over the August figure) and the change in the same month of the previous year (March 2002 compared to March 2001).

Finally, detailed PPI figures break down producer price information not just by the stage of processing (raw, intermediate and finished) but also by industry.

Recent changes

In the UK, PPI information for one month is generally published around seven to ten days after the start of the following month. Table 4.7 shows some changes in 2001 and early 2002.

Interpretation

Different PPI numbers have different significance. Over a long period (several decades) a pattern can be seen in statistics like this that makes more obvious their limitations for forecasting.

Table 4.7 UK producer prices statistics

Output prices (home sales)				
	All manufactured products		Excluding food, beverages, tobacco and petroleum	
	Percentage change over:		Percentage change over:	
	12 months	1 month*	12 months	1 month*
2001 September	−0.2	0.1	0.0	0.0
October	−0.6	−0.2	−0.1	0.0
November	−1.4	−0.7	0.1	0.0
December	−1.1	0.1	0.0	−0.1
2002 January	−0.6	0.1	0.1	0.0
February	−0.2	0.2	0.1	0.0
March	−1.3	0.1	0.0	0.0

*not seasonally adjusted

Source: National Statistics

In general terms, the closer the statistic to the final customer, the less volatile it is. So prices of raw materials – including fuel, commodities, feedstock chemicals and materials used in manufacturing – are the most volatile. Prices of intermediate goods and components are less volatile, while prices of finished goods are the least volatile. However, even producer prices for finished goods tend to be more volatile than retail prices, partly because some of the differences in price will be absorbed in retailer stocks and their profit margins. Retailers may reason that it is not worth passing on small variations in the cost of goods they sell to the consumer.

In the US and UK alike, most analysts look at the total figures for all finished manufactured goods and at those for consumer goods, and those excluding food and energy (in the UK it's food, drink, tobacco and energy). One reason for stripping out food and energy is that prices here tend to be more unpredictable. Rightly or wrongly, analysts sometimes call this component of the PPI the 'core' rate of producer price inflation.

One point worth remembering is that in modern economies with a high service component, producer prices for manufactured goods are not telling the whole story.

Why is it important for you?

The PPI is usually taken to be a lead indicator of retail price inflation. But to view it just in this light is really a gross oversimplification – comparing apples and pears.

Why? Because the PPI includes capital goods as well as consumer goods, whereas retail price indices typically also include services, which PPI figures exclude. Detailed statistics on PPI contain separate statistics for prices of consumer products, but it's worth remembering that probably around half of the RPI is not actually represented in the consumer component of the PPI.

Another point is that the PPI's power as a means of forecasting future rates of retail price inflation is that, to the extent that PPI component increases are passed on by retailers to consumers, the price changes are passed on quickly and therefore often appear in the same month's figures.

Yet inflation is also affected by a range of other factors, including the competitive situation in the retail marketplace, the general level of retail sales, whether or not the economy is functioning at or below full capacity, and other factors that lie completely outside the scope of the PPI.

Sustained increases (or decreases) in the PPI may, however, be an indicator in general terms that inflationary (or deflationary) pressures are building up. As a result it may produce economic policy moves that have a more direct impact on our collective pocket, such as rising interest rates and tighter credit. At the other end of the scale, weak PPI data, together with other factors, may encourage the central bank to relax monetary conditions and cut interest rates to attempt to produce a revival in the economy. Recent trends have suggested that deflation is more of a risk than inflation.

Input prices, industry's own costs, are useful as a way of predicting future trends in the prices that producers may attempt to charge for the products they manufacture. But there is little attention paid in the media to this aspect of the PPI figures. The figures often show sharp variations.

Fuel, crude oil, imported metals and chemicals, all of which can vary significantly in price from month to month, make up in total just under half the index. Yearly changes well into double figures (up or down) are not uncommon for some of these.

In short, PPI contain quite a lot of useful information, but much of it is not glamorous or neatly packaged into a number that analysts and commentators can relate to easily. The result is that some of the detail tends to get lost. Commentators are often quick to trumpet any change in any inflation rate as news, even if it isn't.

IN BRIEF

- Inflation is measured by the RPI in the UK and by the CPI in the US.
- Inflation indices like this are not necessarily a true measure of the cost of living for each individual.
- Money supply is a key indicator for overall economic activity. It refers to anything that can be accepted as payment, including both cash and bank credit.
- Money supply is within the control of the central banks and statistics on money supply often give a good indication of where the economy is headed.
- PPIs are an alternative measure of inflation in the economy as a whole.
- Because of its sharper fluctuations, the PPI has limitations for economic forecasting.

What we spend

What we spend is a vital force that drives the economy. But spending has several facets. It's tempting to see spending purely in terms of what we, as consumers, do when we go shopping. But overall spending is influenced by what the government spends and what businesses spend.

Consumer spending is one of the most critical economic variables, not least because it drives the output of goods and services across large sections of the economy. Because we spend, we generate the production of the goods and services we want to buy, we generate employment at the firms that produce those products and at the shops where we buy them.

Consumer spending thrives when consumers are confident. If consumer confidence is lacking, spending will wilt. Consumer confidence depends on us being secure in our jobs, generally optimistic about the course of the economy, and happy that the other assets we own are maintaining or increasing their value.

Consumers often finance their spending by credit. So we need to be sure that credit is widely available. We also need to know that the assets we can count on to offset that credit are not dropping in value. If we feel nervous, we may want to reduce our borrowings by cutting spending. If credit is expensive or in short supply, we may be forced to consume less.

Spending by companies is another vital ingredient. Companies generally spend most productively on new capital investment. They do this in order to make themselves more efficient at serving customers. They also invest through working capital, extending credit to customers and making sure they have sufficient stocks to supply demand. Some of what companies spend may, however, go unrecorded in official data. This is because it will be in the form of investment to support intangible assets such as intellectual property and brand names.

> Consumer spending thrives when consumers are confident. If consumer confidence is lacking, spending will wilt.

Finally, public spending, financed by governments through taxation, is also an important component in the overall economy. Governments spend on defence, on infrastructure and on social benefits. In turn this feeds through to spending by the recipients. Government spending has been used on a number of occasions to stimulate sluggish economic activity.

Statistics for all these components can show us exactly how the economy is functioning and what is happening to the overall level of demand for goods and services within it.

Consumer spending

Definition

Consumer spending is personal expenditure by individuals and households on goods and services. In a strict sense it differs from consumption. This is because goods that are purchased on a particular day or in a particular month may be consumed over a period of days, months or even years. Consumer spending is always presented in the statistics in money terms, or as percentage changes.

Alternative names

Consumer spending is sometimes called consumer expenditure, personal expenditure, private consumption and occasionally by other names. Don't confuse it with consumer confidence, which is a different thing entirely.

How it's calculated

In the UK, consumer spending figures are compiled and published quarterly as part of a broader set of statistics on GDP. GDP is widely used shorthand for the overall size of the economy. It is the total value of all the goods and services produced by individuals and companies in the domestic economy.

In the US and some other markets, the statistics appear monthly. Statistics on consumer spending are prone to error and are often revised.

The statistics on UK consumer spending are presented in a variety of ways. There are figures for spending at market prices and at constant prices. Figures for spending at constant prices in the UK are currently (in 2002) based on 1995 prices. This means that any subsequent change in consumer spending has been adjusted ('deflated' in the jargon) to remove the effects of inflation quarter by quarter in the intervening period. Data is also provided on a seasonally adjusted basis.

The items that do and don't enter the statistics on consumer spending are:

■ IN:
  – implied benefit from living in your own home
  – income in kind
  – administration of life and pensions.

■ OUT:
  – interest on consumer credit
  – purchase of property
  – buying second-hand goods.

There are several quirks in the figures in terms of what is and what isn't counted as consumer spending. For example, if you live in your own home, as many of us do, the statisticians will calculate what you might have spent in rent to live in an equivalent property and add this amount to the total.

The same is true if you receive income in kind. They will calculate the amount you would have needed to spend to produce an income of this amount in money terms. The costs of administering life assurance and pensions are also calculated and included, even though these costs are normally hidden in premiums.

On the other hand, what you might pay out in interest is excluded, even though you might have financed your spending through credit. Purchases of property are also excluded. Spending on second-hand goods is also excluded from the statistics, on the grounds that it represents a payment for transfer of ownership and not new production.

There is a similar regime in the US. But there data on personal income and expenditure appears both monthly as separate indicators and in the normal quarterly GDP statistics as in the UK. In the US, as in the UK, data comes both in raw form and with various adjustments, including ones that strip out seasonal variations and the effects of inflation. The monthly report in the US appears to give somewhat more information as regards the industries and sectors where money is spent. In the UK, detailed information is compiled in the annual Family Expenditure Survey.

Recent changes

In the UK the data on consumer spending appears in the quarterly GDP report. This is published approximately seven weeks after the end of the quarter in question. Hence first-quarter figures appear towards the end of May, second-quarter figures towards the end of August and so on. Table 5.1 shows changes in the UK between 1999 and 2001.

In the US, the monthly data series comes out during the fourth week following the end of the month in question.

Interpretation

In the UK, because the figures for consumer expenditure appear somewhat in arrears, the value of the data is not as great as it might be. Like most statistics, it is backward looking. In addition, the quarterly published figures show trends only in broad categories by way of a commentary in the background notes accompanying the releases. A sentence or two identifies the main areas of growth and decline.

In the US, the figures show a more detailed analysis of spending split between durable goods, non-durables and services, with several subcategories within each grouping.

Because the figures are history by the time they are published, one needs to beware of drawing too many conclusions from them. This makes life difficult: consumer spending is one of the main influences on the economy. But consumers are fickle and patterns of spending one month may not be reflected in the following month or quarter.

Table 5.1 Statistics on UK consumer spending

Final consumer expenditure by households		Current prices	Constant prices
1999	Q1	139218	127387
	Q2	140945	128751
	Q3	142635	129904
	Q4	144757	131715
2000	Q1	146808	133180
	Q2	147782	134071
	Q3	149395	135225
	Q4	151251	136523
2001	Q1	152747	137574
	Q2	155884	139057
	Q3	158236	140568
	Q4	160090	142173
% change:			
on prior quarter		1.1	0.9
on same quarter of prior year		5.8	4.1

Source: National Statistics

The fact that the figures are revised frequently also argues for not taking too much notice of any quarter's figures. At least, it means not basing your investment decisions on one set of figures alone. That said, the figures for percentage change in real consumer spending (that is, the figures at constant prices) are the best guide to what's going on.

To counter the problem of the figures being backward looking, one solution is to use consumer spending data in conjunction with other indicators, notably surveys of consumer confidence. These are more subjective and anecdotal. If done scientifically and interpreted carefully, however, they can give a greater insight into the current thinking of consumers. They help you estimate whether or not consumption in the immediate future is likely to increase or decrease.

Another way is to follow the patterns between different industries that have held good in the past. Retail sales of all types of goods tend to lead the changes in broader consumer spending, as do car sales.

Why is it important for you?

In most countries consumer spending represents between 60% and 70% of GDP. It follows that changes in consumer spending have a big impact on the underlying rate of economic growth. If consumers feel nervous and insecure, or feel that the other components of their wealth (such as the value of their home or their investments) are falling or likely to fall, they may decide to save more of their income rather than spend it.

Governments can influence this up to a point by reducing interest rates and by making credit cheaper and more readily available. Low interest rates reduce the attractiveness of saving, and easier credit makes consumers worry less about being able to finance their spending.

But spending has to be seen in the context of the overall level of debt in the economy, and the prevailing political and economic climate. If the outlook is bleak, precautionary saving may rise even if rates are very low. Lowering rates and easing credit alone cannot make people spend.

Paradoxically, heavy consumer spending in a recession – the reverse of what one might expect – may prompt the authorities to postpone planned interest rate cuts for fear of stoking a spending boom still more.

Influences on spending are sometimes the opposite to what one might expect. One reason for this is that overlaying people's normal desire to spend their income is a life-cycle pattern. New households and the elderly tend to spend more heavily, while those in middle age tend to have surplus income at their disposal, or possibly even inheritances that they can invest and save for retirement.

In the depths of recession consumers may eat into their savings to maintain their spending. But in the early part of a downturn they are as likely to save – that is, postpone spending – because of increasing uncertainty. Overlaying this is the simple fact that consumers may have fully extended their credit in the boom and hence not have savings to dip into even if they wanted to.

Paradoxically, when inflation is rising, people tend to save more and spend less. In fact, the opposite would be a more rational course of action. A better plan would be to borrow to make purchases now, taking advantage of lower prices and letting inflation erode the future burden of the debt.

Consumer confidence

Definition

Definitions vary, but the meaning is clear. How confident are consumers about the current and likely future outlook to spend and continue spending? Do those expecting to continue or to increase their spending outweigh those of a gloomier disposition?

> Confidence is an elusive concept.

Confidence is an elusive concept. We may think we know it when we see it, but for consumers to hand cash or credit cards over the shop counter is the only way to know for sure.

Alternative names

All consumer confidence measurements are based on surveys rather like opinion polls. Specialist pollsters conduct them on a scientific basis. Usually they do not have an axe to grind in the outcome.

In the US, the Conference Board, a long-established consulting firm, produces monthly figures for consumer confidence, as does Gallup. In the UK, MORI produces similar figures. GfK, a German market research company, produces consumer confidence data – among a range of other statistics – for the European Commission. In Japan there is the Tanken survey.

In addition, investment banks, trade organizations and other groups periodically commission surveys relating to consumer behaviour. In the UK, for example, the Consumers Association produces a quarterly consumer trends survey. In the US, an alternative indicator used comes from the University of Michigan's Survey Research Centre. The Michigan survey produces figures for consumer expectations based around an index number with a base period in the first quarter of 1966.

How it's calculated

Calculating consumer confidence indicators is done through interviews with a random sample of consumers. The sample aims to produce a result that is representative of attitudes in the country as a whole, and of the population structure. In other words it is a stratified random sample weighted for differing income groups, occupations and areas of the country.

Results can be presented in a variety of ways: one is an index number with a base some time in the past. Here, it is the percentage change in the index from month to month or by comparison with the same period in the previous year that is the important parameter.

An alternative method of presenting the data is where the questions are structured to produce clear-cut answers, to use the 'balance of those expecting an improvement' concept, by subtracting (or dividing) the percentage expecting a pessimistic outcome from (or by) the percentage expecting an optimistic one. In this instance, the result is looked at in absolute terms, with the change from one month to the next being the significant one. The point to make is to use the indicators to spot a change in trend. Hence a swing from an indicator of −15 to −5 might be construed as positive whereas the indicator falling from +20 to +10 would be evidence of deteriorating sentiment.

S I D E B A R

How confidence surveys work

The method used by the Conference Board is a good example of the way consumer confidence surveys work. The board sends out a questionnaire each month to a representative sample of 5000 households, of which around 3500 usually respond. Different households are used each month.

The questions have remained constant throughout the history of the index, which originated in 1967. They include questions on general business conditions, employment conditions and income.

Respondents can reply in one of three ways: positive, negative and neutral. In the case of each question the positive figure is divided by the negative figure to get the relative value, which is then compared with the value established for 1985, the base year for the index.

Different index values are calculated using some or all of the resulting sub-indices. The index for consumer confidence, for example, is the average of the index numbers of responses to all five questions asked. Indices for the two questions relating to current business and employment conditions are averaged to get the 'present situation' number.

The remaining three questions, which relate to expectations, form the basis for the 'expectations' indicator.

The consumer confidence barometer produced by GfK for the European Commission (which includes separate indicators for the UK) is calculated in broadly the same way but with a sample size of around 2000 and a broader range of questions. Data runs from 1982 and the survey has been undertaken continuously since the 1970s.

Results appear in different ways, but the one most often publicized appears to be given by subtracting the balance of neutral and negative answers from positive ones. This results in a long-term average figure for Euro-zone consumer confidence in the region of −12. As noted earlier, the absolute number is less important than the direction of the trend or any change in trend.

Recent changes

Table 5.2 shows figures for UK and US consumer confidence at the end of 2001.

Interpretation

As with many statistics, one needs to beware of placing too much attention on a single month's figures. With confidence numbers, it's worth also bearing in mind that although the calculation is performed in a consistent way, the responses to the questionnaire can be erratic and might be taken on a day when the headline news has been particularly optimistic or pessimistic. Consumers are fickle.

However, one interesting aspect of surveys like this is that they tap into the pulse of the economy well before the influences in question have an impact on official published statistics. One source describes the confidence surveys as the best real-time information on consumer spending you can get.

Table 5.2 Consumer confidence statistics

	GfK consumer confidence barometer			Conference board		
		Change on:				
	Dec 01	Month	Year		Dec 01	Nov 01
Personal finances	Plus 6	Up 1	Up 3	Consumer confidence	93.7	84.9
PF expectations	Plus 12	Up 3	Up 1	Present situation	96.9	96.2
General economy	Minus 19	N/c	Down 4	Expectations	91.5	77.3
Overall	Minus 18	Up 8	Down 9			

Source: GfK; Conference Board

Another point is that because they reflect the views of consumers on the ground, it may be that they are more sensitive to shifts in economic conditions, with respondents reacting to and picking up subtle shifts in the economic environment well before they become apparent to policymakers.

The statistical methods used in the surveys can produce sharp swings in the numbers since they very often take the difference between two variables.

S I D E B A R

How the numbers can swing – a fictional example

The University of Ruritania produces the Rassendyl monthly consumer confidence index by sampling 100 households.

Last month it recorded responses as follows:

10% neutral, 60% positive and 30% negative.

Result: a figure of +30 is recorded for consumer confidence by subtracting the negative percentage from the positive one.

This month the results are:

10% neutral, 50% positive, 40% negative.

The overall result drops from +30 to +10.

In other words, only ten households have switched from being positive to being negative, but the difference has fallen sharply.

A shift of one-sixth of the previously positive households into the opposite category produces a drop of two-thirds in the index figure.

Another problem is that consumer confidence cannot really be viewed in isolation. Having an economy full of confident consumers at a time when consumer credit is fully extended and savings are at a low ebb is all very well but may indicate overconfidence. It will not necessarily produce a sustained economic stimulus – because consumers may run out of money to spend, however much they may want to go on shopping.

The danger in a situation like this, as was the case in the US in 2001, is that a blow to confidence will be magnified as less confident consumers respond by running down credit, rebuilding their balance sheets and saving more, producing a sharp (albeit possibly temporary) drop in spending.

This is the danger in measuring consumer confidence numbers against levels seen at the peaks and troughs of previous cycles. Other conditions – savings rates interest rates and credit availability – may not have been the same then. Expecting the consumer confidence number to be the same may be unwise.

Why is it important for you?

However imperfect, consumer confidence numbers are important because they are leading indicators – they show which way the economy is moving before it is reflected in the official statistics. The more confident consumers are, the more likely they are to spend in future and thereby boost the economy.

Because consumer spending is such an important influence on the economy, consumer confidence indicators that show confidence at a high level may encourage policymakers to take pre-emptive action to stop the economy from overheating. By the same token, depressed consumer spending may call for an economic stimulus to get things moving back in the right direction.

Measurement of consumer confidence can also be done through other forms of indicator. Some of these are more popular in conditions that produce both economic slowdown and relatively high rates of inflation, such as were apparent in the 1970s. These indicators are often called 'misery indices', as they are likely to coincide with pessimism on the part of the consumer.

One measure of the general level of misery is the rate of inflation plus the unemployment rate. Another misery index is price inflation plus interest rates. In both cases, the higher the index is, the more miserable consumers are likely to be.

Public spending

Definition

Public spending is what the government spends on our behalf, on defence, infrastructure, social security and paying interest on government debt. Official statistics distinguish between current spending, on social benefits, public sector wages and general running costs, and capital spending (or investment) in capital projects.

Alternative names

The distinction between current spending and capital spending needs to be kept in mind. Some statistics also use the concept of 'government consumption' to measure what governments buy from outside the public sector. And spending is only half of the equation. The government funds its spending from taxes on the income and spending of individuals and businesses.

The public sector borrowing requirement (PSBR) is another term often bandied around by commentators. In broad terms it reflects the balance between government receipts on the one hand and public spending, both current spending and capital investment, on the other. In the UK in 1998/99, 1999/00 and 2000/01, the balance was a surplus rather than a deficit and the government was able to reduce borrowings.

How it's calculated

Public spending shows up in the UK's statistics in two forms. National Statistics publishes a monthly release on public sector finances. This provides data on the public sector in a conventional accounting framework, that is, including data on income and expenditure, interest payments, capital spending, depreciation, surpluses and deficits. Other than a small depreciation element, public sector accounting is primarily presented as a cash flow statement.

Government spending also crops up as part of the GDP figures, issued quarterly. This shows figures for general government spending as part of the final consumption expenditure figures. The figures differ considerably from the current expenditure figures shown in the public sector accounts.

At the time of writing, for example, a quarter's current expenditure as shown in the public sector finance release amounted to £85bn, whereas the same quarter's numbers in the GDP release showed spending at £45bn. The explanation for the difference is that the GDP figures represent mainly third-party expenditure on goods and services and don't include transfer payments such as social security. So there is a fairly close, although not exact, match between the public sector accounts view of current expenditure excluding interest and social benefits, and the GDP figure for spending.

The same dichotomy is present in public sector spending in the US and in other countries. In America, for example, in GDP figures government spending is categorized as consumption expenditure and investment. Differences between these figures and those in the government accounts reflect several factors: transfers to other public entities, grants, such as foreign aid, interest and subsidies for state-owned companies and any spending that is not defined as being 'for current use'.

The reason for mentioning this in such detail is that a plethora of definitions and alternative ways of presenting the figures can give rise to confusion. They allow the unscrupulous to use the numbers to make partisan political or propaganda points that the statistics themselves do not really support.

Public spending totals are usually shown in terms of current prices. That is to say, they include the effects of inflation. Stripping out inflation is no easy task because inflation in public sector spending may be at a somewhat different rate to the 'deflators' (the multipliers used to get to the inflation-adjusted figures) that are normally used.

Finally, international comparisons are complicated by the fact that different countries make up their public sector accounts using different financial year-ends. Just as companies have different fiscal years, so do governments. In the UK, Canada and Japan, the year is 31 March. In the US, it is 30 September. Just to complicate things, the UK's GDP-based figures for government spending are added up on a calendar-year basis.

Table 5.3 offers a quick analysis of what some governments spend our money on.

Recent changes

Table 5.4 shows figures for UK public spending between 1999 and 2001 taken from the quarterly national accounts.

Table 5.3 What governments spend

	UK	France	Germany	Italy	Spain
Defence	15	16	7	10	9
Law and order	10	5	8	10	13
Education	24	26	19	30	23
Health	22	17	33	20	25
Social security	27	8	17	4	5
Housing	2	7	2	3	5
Other	0	21	14	23	20
Total	100	100	100	100	100
% of GDP	21.1	19.8	19.9	16.3	16.7

Source: The Economist

Table 5.4 Statistics on UK public spending

		General government expenditure	
		Current prices	Constant prices
1999	Q1	40889	37085
	Q2	41229	37104
	Q3	41793	37309
	Q4	42383	37562
2000	Q1	42662	37642
	Q2	43748	38046
	Q3	44470	38250
	Q4	44558	37979
2001	Q1	45487	38618
	Q2	46525	38921
	Q3	46965	39183
	Q4	48883	39753
% change			
on prior quarter		3.3	1.4
on same quarter of prior year		7.7	3.0

Source: National Statistics

Interpretation

Public sector accounts are generally fairly transparent to those with a basic knowledge of accounting. However, the most closely watched statistics are those for central government, whereas the public sector as a whole includes local government and public corporations. In broad terms, however, over the years the cash requirements of central government and the public sector as a whole have generally been of the same order of magnitude.

Just like businesses, cash requirements and borrowings can differ quite widely from time to time because of leads and lags in payments and receipts. In other words, the government's working capital can fluctuate just like that of a business.

In general terms it's always worthwhile comparing the monthly figures with those of several previous months and years. Government spending tends to be at a fairly constant rate. Government receipts are a different matter. For example, tax receipts do not accrue particularly evenly. There are big peaks in January and July for income tax and in January, April, July and October for corporation tax.

Another point worth watching is the predilection of governments from time to time to massage the figures by changing definitions – shifting some items to the capital account to make current spending look more modest, for example. Equally, some items traditionally included as current spending, on education or on defence equipment, for example, might more honestly be classified as capital investment since they are made with an eye to the future.

> Another point worth watching is the predilection of governments from time to time to massage the figures by changing definition.

One-off receipts can also influence the figures. Obvious examples are privatization and similar receipts such as those from the auction of the third-generation mobile phone spectrum. These can distort things not only for the months in which they occur but also in subsequent years when they may influence comparisons.

Why is it important for you?

Well-controlled public spending is an indicator of good government. Governments cannot avoid spending. One may quibble over the efficiency with which it is spent and the priorities in the spending totals, but a certain level of social spending is vital to the well-being of a modern society and properly functioning economy. Social benefits account for about 30% of all government spending, interest payments 7.5% and the balance is made up of other current spending.

Expressed as a percentage of GDP, general government spending in the UK, when adjusted to include social benefit payments, is just under 40% of the total. Government debt is around 30% of GDP. Relative to other European countries, with some exceptions, Britain spends above average on defence and public order and below average on education.

From the standpoint of investors, changes in the patterns of public spending may be more important than the overall totals. Government documents and statistical publications are well worth reading to try and gauge whether or not there are companies that may benefit from changes in policy.

S I D E B A R

Government spending as a policy instrument

In earlier eras governments used public spending to stimulate the economy. The best example was the creation of the Tennessee Valley Authority, one of the measures that helped to lift the US economy out of the depression by providing jobs and incomes in an otherwise depressed area.

Deficit spending, using public expenditure to stimulate the economy, even if it meant running a budget deficit, was a policy prescription advocated by the economist John Maynard Keynes in the inter-war period. In the past 20 years or so this has fallen into disuse. Governments have preferred to use monetary policy and interest rates as their main tools for providing economic stimulus. The result is that observing trends in public spending may give fewer clues to likely trends in the economy in the future than it once did.

Having said that, and notwithstanding its right-wing complexion, the Bush government in the US has been keen to employ the stimulus of public sector spending to revive the economy in the wake of the shock to the economic system administered by the terrorist attacks on the World Trade Center in September 2001. The package was deemed necessary particularly as, at that point at least, the stimulus supplied by easier monetary conditions did not seem to be having the desired effect. The effect was blunted because much of the money went direct to companies rather than to individual consumers.

So while nominally at least balanced budgets and repayment of public debt are seen to be virtues, events on the world stage may conspire to knock governments off their avowed path of fiscal rectitude.

Deficit spending of the sort advocated by Keynes, until recently reviled, has been accepted back into the fold as a legitimate policy choice. Cultured British aesthete Keynes meets Texan rancher Bush. An odd couple indeed.

Investors, especially conservative ones, need not lament rising government spending too seriously. Government deficits, provided they are kept within modest bounds and do not stoke inflation, mean a bigger supply and greater variety of high-quality government bonds.

It seems likely, in light of recent trends in the US economy, for example, that the vaunted abandonment of new issues of the 30-year bond does not signal the permanent demise of the 'long bond', but merely its hibernation. Governments in the US and elsewhere will sooner or later (and possibly even sooner than they expect) find the need to finance spending by means of cheap, long-dated bond issues. This pushes the problems of keeping today's economy in balance onto the next generation.

Business spending

Definition

Business spending means purchases of fixed assets to use in a business. Companies invest in buildings – offices and factories – and in equipment – machinery, computers and office furniture. They do it to make themselves more productive. They aim to get a payback on the investment.

Business investment also takes in the capital committed to stocks of finished goods and raw materials. In the official statistics in the UK this shows up in the quarterly figures for GDP, alongside consumer spending and general government spending.

Capital spending by companies is known as gross domestic fixed capital formation. This is a long-winded phrase. What it means is that the investment is counted before depreciation is deducted, that it is for businesses in the home country (i.e. domestic) and that it is a fixed capital item rather than a financial commitment. Changes in stocks (or inventories) are also regarded as part of fixed capital formation.

Alternative names

In popular usage, gross domestic fixed capital formation goes by several other names – fixed investment, capital investment, capital spending, and additions to capital stock. Inventories are interchangeable with stocks in terms of their meaning. In the US, terms that normally in the UK might be called plant and machinery are called non-residential structures and producers' durable equipment.

How it's calculated

Data on fixed investment is part of the quarterly GDP figures. Usually the figures are stated both in nominal money terms at current prices and on a constant price basis, that is, after removing the effects of inflation. The data used to arrive at these figures derives primarily from business surveys and occasionally also from industry data.

Inventory levels are arrived at in the same way, but it is important to remember that it is changes in inventories that show up in the GDP numbers, not the absolute level of stocks. Capital formation as a whole normally represents just under 20% of GDP.

Recent changes

Table 5.5 shows figures for UK gross domestic domestic fixed capital formation and changes in inventories between 1999 and 2001.

Table 5.5 Statistics on UK gross fixed capital formation

		Gross domestic fixed capital formation		Changes in inventories	
		Current prices	Constant prices	Current prices	Constant prices
1999	Q1	38411	37586	1138	1541
	Q2	38381	37216	327	384
	Q3	38925	37494	1459	1276
	Q4	39691	38170	2051	1776
2000	Q1	39463	37928	224	266
	Q2	41253	39044	573	840
	Q3	41335	39683	1021	1072
	Q4	43197	41111	37	272
2001	Q1	41809	39741	1624	1552
	Q2	43444	40701	293	79
	Q3	42486	39859	641	260
	Q4	41544	39149	−706	−561
% change:					
on prior quarter		−1.3	0.7		
on same quarter of prior year		−3.1	−4.0		

Source: National Statistics

Interpretation

All of the components of GDP given in official statistics should be regarded as estimates. In the UK, the press releases from National Statistics note that 'estimates are given to the nearest million, but cannot be regarded as accurate to this degree'. The assumption made by most forecasters is that if the method of collecting the data remains consistent, then the error level in each set of data should be more or less constant, and so percentage changes and comparisons based on the data will be little affected.

As assumptions go, this may be a little suspect, although it must be said that forecasters perhaps pay less attention to figures for business investment than they do to overall figures for GDP, consumer spending, the PSBR and inflation.

The data for fixed capital investment in recent years shows a steady upward trend but this cannot be assumed to be the case for ever.

Data is often revised as new information comes to light, so making over-much of one month's figures may be unwise. In general, though, business investment is likely to be cyclical.

Since the reason for investing in this way is generally to increase capacity or to make a business more efficient, if the economy is sluggish or declining, the incentive to do this is less and, moreover, companies may be more in a mood to conserve cash.

Capital investment projects frequently have a long lead time (although for many industries these days less of a lead time than was once the case), so cancelling investment may not show up in the statistics for some time. Inventories are likely to be more sensitive. If a drop in demand catches a business by surprise, the result will be higher inventories initially. Production will then be cut back, possibly to below the level of demand, and inventories run down before production levels are reinstated. Hence changes in inventories can be a sensitive guide to the state of business.

The advent of modern service-based economies has to some degree reduced the importance of fixed capital formation and inventory spending in the overall scheme of things. When businesses are providing services based on the knowledge possessed by their workers rather than on their physical labour supplemented by machinery, the change in the role of capital investment is obvious.

Because of the long lead time for capital investment and the volatile nature of movements in stocks, there are better guides to the current and future spending intentions of the corporate sector. These generally take the form of indicators from individual industries that are known to be sensitive to economic conditions or spending by companies, such as new housing construction, car sales, imports of capital goods and so on.

In most advanced economies there are also regular surveys of business's investment intentions. These parallel the surveys conducted on consumer spending. They are covered in more detail in the next chapter.

Why is it important for you?

Fixed investment by businesses might be assumed to be the bedrock of the economy, but in reality many businesses these days spend more on intellectual property and other intangible assets than they do on physical assets.

By their very nature intangible assets are hard to measure with any degree of accuracy, may face sudden obsolescence (though their owners would rarely admit this) and hence are difficult to include in official statistics in any meaningful way. Corporate spending on advertising, for example, may have assumed more importance in businesses, as advertising and sales promotion is employed to protect and enhance the value of brands.

S I D E B A R

Capital formation and pharma

Drug companies are an interesting case in point for capital formation. They are huge businesses and generate massive levels of sales and a high return on capital. Yet the foundations of pharma companies are built on patents and marketing.

Though they have teams of scientists and high-powered laboratories, and spend heavily on research and development of new drugs, this spending is dwarfed by what they spend paying teams of salesmen, known in the trade as 'detailers', and in marketing their products through awareness programmes with doctors, and even consumer advertising.

Other than what they might spend on building gleaming head offices, the fixed capital spending that these big multinational companies might make, in terms of what might show up in official statistics, hugely understates their real size in terms of market power, economic influence and political clout.

The other basic point is that, measured conventionally, gross domestic fixed capital formation is a comparatively minor component of GDP, currently around 18% in the UK. This means that changes in the numbers and in corporate investment intentions are much less significant than they are for example for consumer spending. Similarly, while the intention of those investing in new equipment may be to improve productivity and efficiency, the result may simply be to create surplus capacity.

In the late 1990s the spending boom was predicated on the rise of the new economy. Vast sums were spent on internet and telecoms infrastructure that may, in the short term at least, prove to have been money down the drain. The idea that it would fuel productivity-led growth has been shown, for the most part, to be a sham.

A final point is that in the past government spending and business spending have to some extent been seen as competitors for resources. If governments choose to subsidize industries they favour or which are in the public sector (rail transport in the UK is a topical example), they must take care. One fear is of siphoning resources from legitimate business spending that may have a better case for allocation of resources.

In this case, investors may opt to finance a government-guaranteed project, even though the economic case for it is unsound, crowding out better ideas that emanate from the private sector but appear riskier.

IN BRIEF

- Consumer spending and consumer confidence are two different things.
- The value of the consumer spending data is not as great as it might be, as the figures are issued significantly in arrears.
- Consumer spending is a big influence on economic growth.
- Consumer confidence is measured by opinion surveys. It is useful for spotting a change in trends.
- Public spending is the money the government spends on our behalf. Well-controlled spending indicates good government.
- Business spending is a comparatively minor component of the GDP and as such is not a significant indicator used in isolation.

chapter six

The work we do

Counterbalancing what we spend both as consumers and businesses is the work we do and what we produce. Some of the statistics produced under this heading have cropped up in earlier chapters.

GDP is a measure of the value of the goods and services produced in the domestic economy (that is, it excludes any foreign trade). But it is also commonly used to measure the overall size of the economy. The phrase 'economic growth', for example, usually means the year-on-year change in GDP.

Industrial production measures just that – the scale of and changes in the production of physical goods. It also includes electricity generation and the use of natural resources. Figures for manufacturing output exclude the output of natural resources and utilities.

In an economy like the UK or US, focusing on industrial production can be misleading. Britain and America are service economies. Much of the value generated in the economy is in the form of services rather than things.

As a writer I make my living generating books and articles. This is intellectual property, the rights to which I sell to my publisher. The publisher produces the physical item – a book or newspaper. But my part in the process is to produce a service.

In the previous chapter we saw that consumer confidence plays a big part in how consumer spending moves on a month-by-month basis. The same is true of businesses. Business confidence is a key barometer that affects how willing companies are to take on more workers, or whether they will be retrenching. It also governs how likely or otherwise they are to invest.

As a small business, if I'm feeling confident about my workload for the next six months, I might take on a school leaver to do some filing and general office work. If things are looking tricky, I might put off buying a new computer or photocopier.

One of the main factors affecting the way consumers feel about life is whether or not they have a job. Figures for unemployment are an important market barometer and have an effect on consumer confidence and in turn consumer spending. The less sure we feel about our jobs, the more cautious we are likely to be in our spending. We might save more to give ourselves a nest egg if we lose our jobs.

Data on output and employment levels can be combined to calculate productivity. This is output per hour worked or per employee. Productivity growth is an important factor in allowing the economy to grow without precipitating inflation.

Gross domestic product

Definition

GDP measures the value of the output of goods and services produced within a country, irrespective of whether or not the businesses in question, or the labour or capital involved, are foreign owned. If something's produced in a country, its value shows up in that country's GDP.

Alternative names

GDP is an almost universal measure for the size of an economy. 'Economic growth' and 'GDP growth' are generally assumed to be one and the same. Press comment uses the terms interchangeably.

GNP, now usually called gross national income (GNI), conveys roughly the same meaning. It is GDP plus net income – rent, interest, profits and dividends – earned abroad. In many economies the two figures are so close as to be almost identical. Net national income (NNI) is GNP minus depreciation. In other words it is GNP after an adjustment has been made to reflect that a proportion of productive assets wear out each year and need to be replaced.

When statisticians compare the GDP figures of different countries, it is common for them to be presented in terms of US dollars. 'Dollar GDP' is an international measure of the size of a country's economy.

How it's calculated

There are two ways of arriving at GDP. One is by totting up the various items of spending in the economy: consumption, investment, government spending, spending of foreigners on exports from the country, minus the spending by us on goods imported from abroad. Goods foreigners buy from us (exports) mean that money is coming in from abroad to pay for goods produced here. To balance this up, we must also count goods we buy that are produced outside the country. This is spending that benefits someone else's economy and leaks out of our own.

The other way of calculating GDP is to look at income derived from everything or everyone involved in producing it. This is called GDP 'at factor cost'. This means the wages and salaries of employees, the incomes of self-employed people, rent on property, trading profits of companies and the surpluses produced by government-owned businesses. Interest and dividends, pensions and social security payments are not included. This is because they are simply transfers from one part of the economy to another and therefore cancel each other out.

GDP calculated by the expenditure method and GDP at factor cost do not match exactly. Since expenditure includes indirect taxes such as excise duty and VAT and also reflects subsidies, these have to be stripped out to make the two figures agree. Even then the match is rarely exact because of differences in the way the data is collected.

> **GDP calculated by the expenditure method and GDP at factor cost do not match exactly.**

In the UK, another measure has been introduced, called gross value added (GVA). This takes out the effects of taxes and subsidies on finished products, but leaves in some other taxes that businesses bear, such as business rates, because these are reckoned to be a cost of production. Which method is better? You pays your money and takes your choice.

The statistics show figures for GDP at both current prices and at constant prices. In the latter case, in the UK 1995 prices are used. This means that the effect of any changes in prices since 1995 is stripped out of the figures so that the statistics can show growth excluding the effects of inflation.

The price adjustment factor we use to get from so-called nominal GDP (that is, calculated at current prices) to GDP at constant prices is known as the GDP deflator.

This is not the same as the inflation measures we looked at in Chapter 4. Inflation relates solely to changes in consumer prices. Measures of consumer price inflation cover only goods and services bought by consumers and are produced monthly with the weights used in the index changed only occasionally.

In the GDP deflator, by contrast, the coverage is broader – goods and services in the consumer, business, government sectors and for imports and exports. Weightings are often adjusted to take account of changing patterns of spending within the overall GDP number.

The deflator (i.e. the price adjustment factor) used in the GDP calculations is a general measure of the overall level of inflation within an economy. But it doesn't pay to draw too many conclusions from it. This is because it reflects not just price changes but also changes in patterns of spending and the resulting weight given to different items.

Government statisticians acknowledge that some elements of the price deflator have to be estimated, and the ways in which these estimates are produced is a little opaque. Since GDP figures are only issued quarterly, the deflators issued with them are only issued with the same frequency. They are frequently revised.

Recent changes

In the UK the data on GDP is in a quarterly report. This is published about seven weeks after the end of the quarter in question. First-quarter figures are published towards the end of May, second-quarter figures towards the end of August and so on. Table 6.1 shows changes in the UK between 1999 and 2001.

In the US, the final GDP numbers are published quarterly, but monthly estimates are also released and then revised over two successive months. The different estimates are known as the 'advance estimate, the 'preliminary estimate', and the 'final estimate'. Data is published during the fourth week following the end of the month in question.

Table 6.1 Statistics on UK GDP

GDP (index of value –1995 = 100)		Current prices	Constant prices
1999	Q1	122.5	110.3
	Q2	124.3	110.9
	Q3	126.3	112.3
	Q4	128.2	113.2
2000	Q1	128.7	113.7
	Q2	130.8	114.6
	Q3	132.3	115.6
	Q4	133.6	116.3
2001	Q1	135.3	117.1
	Q2	137.3	117.7
	Q3	138.5	118.2
	Q4	139.4	118.0

Source: National Statistics

Interpretation

GDP figures are used as a proxy for the economy as a whole, but the numbers, though widely used, do have their limitations. One is more to do with what is not included. This big omission relates to any work that is unpaid.

When space is hard to fill, newspaper editors often trot out articles about the true economic value of a housewife. It is a fact that unpaid and domestic activities do not show up in GDP, but nonetheless have some value even if it isn't measured. Housewives do not show up in GDP, but if you pay a cleaner, cook and childminder, they would.

Second-hand transactions or the exchange of one good for another (barter or payments in kind) also don't show up. There is a range of intangible costs that aren't measured. Use of irreplaceable natural resources or the costs of environmental pollution are examples.

Some public spending is understated. Spending on services for the community, the police and fire service, for example, are measured largely in terms of wages but arguably contribute more than this in less tangible ways because the population feel safer.

Changes in the quality of goods and services sold do not show up in the figures.

Perhaps the biggest drawback to GDP figures – worse in some countries than others – is the size of the so-called 'black' economy. The black economy refers to unrecorded transactions, usually in cash, that are the result of attempts by either party involved to evade tax or conceal economic activity for other reasons. Estimates of how big a problem this is are largely hearsay. More heavily taxed countries are more susceptible to it. Within Europe, the problem is generally reckoned to be biggest in Italy and probably least marked in Germany, the UK and Switzerland.

The US, where black economy transactions are put at anything from 4% to 33% of the total (all those illegal immigrants in California), attempts to adjust its GDP figures to allow for this figure. Italy does the same. The chances are that both adjustments underestimate the impact of the black economy.

One of the obvious ways in which GDP doesn't tell quite the whole story relates to transfer payments. Interest, dividends, social security payments, gifts, pensions and the like are all classed in this way, because they represent the economy giving with one hand and taking away with the other. Social security payments come out of taxes, pensions come out of past premiums, dividends come out of company profits, and so on.

Yet simply because these are classed as transfer payments does not mean that they aren't important in the context of the economy as a whole. Interest payments are a case in point. Interest costs are an important regulator of economic activity, even if their impact on overall GDP is neutral.

To summarize what's not in GDP:

- unpaid work (e.g. housewives)
- social benefit of emergency services
- second-hand transactions
- any form of payment in kind or barter
- any form of transfer payment (gifts, pensions, dividends, etc.)
- depletion of natural resources
- 'black economy' (unrecorded cash transactions).

Why is it important for you?

It may be that GDP numbers are given an importance they don't deserve. If you work in manufacturing industry or in another business that has been under financial strain, it is probably no consolation that GDP is still growing. Conversely, some individuals enjoy a life of affluence, unaffected by the fact that the economy may be declining.

GDP is an amalgamation of a number of other statistics that make up its different components, many of which are announced more frequently or earlier in the release cycle of monthly and quarterly statistics. It's more than likely that by the time GDP numbers appear, we will have a good idea what they are likely to show.

GDP growth and decline is a good measure of performance and the only one that is in any way comparable internationally. Two successive quarters of declining GDP is supposed to signify a recession. But for many in the front line of business, the chill of an impending recession is often felt well before it shows up in the figures.

This brings us neatly on to business confidence and how it can be measured.

Business confidence

Definition

As with consumer confidence, the meaning of business confidence seems intuitively pretty obvious. How confident are businesses about the current and likely future outlook? How will this affect the employment levels of their businesses and how much they invest? Do those expecting to continue spending or to increase inventories outweigh those of a gloomier disposition? But confidence is nonetheless an elusive concept, hard to pin down precisely.

Alternative names

Like consumer confidence measurements, business confidence measures are based on surveys rather like opinion polls. Specialist pollsters conduct them on a scientific basis. Usually they do not have an axe to grind in the outcome.

There are equivalents in the business sphere to almost every common measure of consumer confidence. In the US, the ISM produces a regular survey that is widely watched. The Conference Board, which also produces consumer confidence numbers, produces a business trends survey. In the UK, the CBI produces a range of similar figures. The Chartered Institute of Purchasing and Supply (CIPS, the UK counterpart to the ISM) produces monthly data. The German IFO index is also widely watched.

Table 6.2 lists the various pollsters

How it's calculated

Calculating business confidence indicators, like consumer confidence numbers, is generally based around interviews with a random sample of businesses. The sample is designed to produce a result that is representative of businesses attitudes in the country as a whole, and of the industrial and size structure of businesses in general. In other words it is a stratified random sample weighted for differing types and sizes of business, and different areas of the country.

Results can be presented in a variety of ways. Often they are shown as an index number with a base sometime in the past. In this case, the percentage change in the index from month to month or by comparison with the same period in the previous year is the important parameter.

An alternative method of presenting the data is where the questions are structured to produce clear-cut answers, to use the 'balance of those expecting an improvement' concept, by subtracting (or dividing) the percentage expecting a pessimistic outcome from (or by) the percentage expecting an optimistic one.

In this instance, the result is looked at in absolute terms, with the change from one month to the next being the significant one. The point is to use the indicators to spot a change in trend. Hence a swing from an indicator of −15

Table 6.2 Business confidence – who are the pollsters?

Country	Pollsters
US	ISM, Conference Board
UK	CBI, CIPS
Germany	IFO
Japan	Bank of Japan

to −5 might be construed as positive whereas the indicator falling from +20 to +10 would be evidence of deteriorating sentiment. Either way you get a single number that is sensitive to shifts in sentiment.

The method used by the Conference Board is a good example of the way these surveys work. It sends out a questionnaire each month to a representative sample of businesses. Different businesses are used each month. As with consumer surveys, not all those surveyed actually respond. The same questions are generally asked each month or each quarter. They include questions on general business conditions, employment, inventories, prices, production and so on. In some countries the content of the surveys differs from month to month or quarter to quarter, although the same things are surveyed at the same time each year.

Results are presented in different ways, but the one most often publicized appears to be given by subtracting the balance of neutral and negative answers from positive ones. As noted earlier, the absolute number is less important than the direction of the trend or any change in trend.

S I D E B A R

ISM – how the system works

Many economists watch the ISM (formerly NAPM) number for changes in economic trends. But the calculations need careful interpretation. Let's look at how they work.

In the case of the US ISM figure, the index is constructed so that the break point is at 50. A figure above 50 indicates strong confidence; a figure below 50 suggests weak confidence.

The index is calculated by asking respondents to assess whether conditions in certain areas of their business are better, worse or the same. The index is calculated by adding the percent expecting an increase to one half of the percent expecting no change. If, for example, 70% of respondents expected no change, 20% expected an improvement and 10% a decline, the index would be 55 (half of 70 = 35 + 20). If 20% expected a decline and 10% an improvement, the index would be 45.

The ISM asks questions based on new orders, production, supplier deliveries, inventories and employment, and weights each component slightly differently to arrive at a composite index. Orders and production levels are deemed relatively more important, inventories and jobs less so.

The ISM isn't alone. The UK's CIPS figure is calculated in a similar way to this.

Table 6.3 Business confidence statistics – UK purchasing managers index

| | Manufacturing | | | Services | | |
	Index	Direction	Rate of change	Index	Direction	Rate of change
	Dec 01	Dec 01		Dec 01	Dec 01	
PMI	45.2	Decrease	Faster	49.4	Decrease	Slower
New orders	47	Decrease	Slower	50.5	Increase	Change of direction
Input prices	40.9	Decrease	Slower	45.7	Decrease	Slower
Quantity of purchases	42.5	Decrease	Faster	49.8	Decrease	Slower
Employment	42	Decrease	Faster	51.1	Increase	Faster

Source: CIPS

Recent changes

Table 6.3 shows figures for UK business confidence in December 2001.

Interpretation

As with many statistics, beware of placing too much attention on a single month's figures. With confidence numbers, it's worth also bearing in mind that although the calculation is performed in a consistent way, the responses to the questionnaire can be erratic and might be taken on a day when the headline news has been particularly optimistic or pessimistic.

That said, respondents to business surveys might, if they take the trouble to respond, answer in a more dispassionate way than consumers.

However, one interesting aspect of surveys like this (the same is true of consumer confidence surveys) is that they tap into the pulse of the economy well before the influences in question have an impact on official published statistics.

It's perhaps exaggerating slightly to say they are real-time, not least because the surveys usually come out a few weeks after the end of the month in question. Given when surveys are sent out and the time taken to collect the responses, the figures may be more backward looking than generally appears.

One big plus, however, is that they reflect the views of real live businesses, coping on a day-to-day basis with order books, payments and receipts, employees and so on. Businesses often feel shifts in the economic climate well before policymakers.

Like consumer surveys, the statistical methods used in business confidence surveys can, by their very nature, produce sharp swings in the numbers. This is because they very often take the difference between two variables or measure the impact of numbers that are essentially views at the margin and can change rapidly.

In the example we gave earlier about the ISM for example, 10% of respondents switching from the positive column to the negative column would be sufficient to produce a pronounced deterioration in the index – certainly one large enough to send Wall Street analysts into a tizzy.

Another problem is that business confidence cannot really be viewed in isolation. Business capital structures – for instance the amount of debt that businesses have on their balance sheets – may have an impact on confidence. If interest rates rise because the policymakers feel that the economy is expanding too fast, businesses may feel threatened, but in a sense that is the very objective that policymakers want to engineer. The flip side is that business people whose wealth is tied up in a buoyant stock market may be generally more optimistic than the conditions warrant.

Business confidence numbers may vary from year to year and may well not be the same as they were at the peaks and troughs of previous cycles. Other conditions – inventory levels, regulation, interest rates, share prices and credit availability – may not have been the same then.

Why is it important for you?

However imperfect, business confidence numbers are important because, like consumer confidence, they are leading indicators – they show which way the economy is moving before it is reflected in the official statistics.

The more confident businesses are, the more likely they are to invest and create jobs, and to spend more on marketing, and thereby boost the economy.

But the degree to which the numbers lead what happens in the real underlying economy does vary. Some economists consider, because of the way the data is collected, that indicators like this are really a mixture of business views about current conditions and those of the future.

> The more confident businesses are, the more likely they are to invest and create jobs, and to spend more on marketing, and thereby boost the economy.

The CBI index of business confidence (calculated taking the difference between the percentages of positive and negative responses) is reckoned to be a solid indicator of the trend in corporate profits about nine months in the future.

Index of production

Definition

The index of production measures the output of those industries that produce specific goods that people buy, as distinct from services. They fall into three broad categories: mining and quarrying (including oil and gas extraction); electricity, water and gas utilities; and manufacturing in the conventional sense.

Alternative names

Manufacturing output is one of the components of the index of production (which used to be called the index of industrial production). In the US, this terminology is still used and the scope of the index is almost identical to the UK's.

How it's calculated

In the UK, the statistics are seasonally adjusted index numbers with a base date of 1995. They measure volume of output. They are produced from returns from the industries concerned. Companies, trade association data and government departments all supply data. In some instances industrial production data is estimated from electric power usage and from labour productivity data provided for employment statistics.

This patchwork of sources suggests that the data, particularly early estimates of monthly numbers, is not as accurate as observers sometimes assume. It is often revised later. As the statistics are refined, figures for production of physical product – what industrial production data is actually supposed to measure – become more readily available and allow more precise statistics to be calculated.

Separate index numbers are compiled for each of the three major categories – manufacturing, mining and utilities – and combined in a composite figure. This composite takes into account the relative importance of the three broad sector groupings. Manufacturing output is the dominant one of the three. Estimates vary, but manufacturing output probably represents about 85% of the total, with the remainder split evenly between mining and utilities. In the UK, detailed index numbers are provided for industry groups on the basis of the Standard Industrial Classification.

Table 6.4 Statistics on UK industrial production

		Production	Extractive	Manufacturing	Utilities
2001	September	103.0	105.1	101.5	114.6
	October	101.5	97.0	101.0	111.2
	November	101.2	96.1	100.3	114.7
	December	100.8	99.9	99.3	113.6
2002	January	100.2	97.5	98.9	114.4
	February	100.0	96.7	99.3	110.0
% change last 3 months:					
on previous 3 months		−1.4	−1.8	−1.4	−0.8
on same period a year ago		−5.1	−0.6	−6.2	0.4
All figures seasonally adjusted: 1995 = 100					

Source: National Statistics

Recent changes

In the UK, the index of production release from National Statistics normally appears around five weeks after the end of the month in question.

Data for 2001 and early 2002 is shown in Table 6.4.

Interpretation

Industrial production is something of a paradox among statistics. It is a good indicator of current economic activity. Yet manufacturing physical goods (as opposed to providing services) is a minority activity in advanced economies.

In America, for example, manufacturing represents only about 20% of GDP. In Germany and Japan the figure is 30% and in the UK somewhere between the two. If utilities and mining are included, the figures rise in both cases by about 10–15 percentage points.

In some countries too (although not in Britain) the index of industrial production does not cover all of industry. In Japan, for example, estimates suggest that around 40% of industrial output is not represented in the index.

Nonetheless stock market statistics watchers pay attention to the numbers. This is because, for all their faults, they do give some clue as to what stage an economy might be at in the business cycle. This claim is becoming harder to justify. In the UK, for example, output has been contracting or stagnant for many years. The current index, for example is identical to the base level of 100 recorded in 1995.

What is often more interesting for observers is the analysis of production figures for broad industrial groups. In the UK statistics' official release, for example, you can see easily in chart form the output of durable goods (cars, washing machines), non-durables (soap, cigarettes), investment goods (machine tools, computers) and intermediate goods (industrial components and the like).

Briefing notes available from National Statistics also highlight any unusual movement in the numbers in any one month, both in general terms and for particular industrial groups.

Why is it important for you?

If you work in or have investments in particular industries it may be worthwhile checking out the figures for output for that industry. The statistics will help you see whether there are any messages either for your job or the sales of companies whose shares you own. The lessons are general ones. Production doesn't always equate to sales, for example.

Several important measures can be derived from production figures, one of which is **productivity**. This is output per employee or output per man-hour. Which measure you choose depends on your preference.

Equally closely followed (particularly in the US, where detailed figures are available) is **capacity utilization**. This is the percentage that current output represents of the maximum sustainable level of production. In other words, what is the level of production that could be consistently maintained for a long period? And what does current output represent as a percentage of it? Companies may be able to produce more than the sustainable maximum on a temporary basis, a reason why some measures of capacity utilization sneak above 100% from time to time.

Capacity utilization typically hovers between 80% and 90%. While this might seem inefficient, a little slack is needed in the system to take account of temporary fluctuations. Working at high levels of production has to be balanced against the extra costs it may create (overtime payments for workers, for instance). High-capacity working may also give rise to pressure for higher wages or tempt manufacturers to put up prices.

One key role of the production figures for economists, however, is to point up changes in individual sectors that can suggest trends in economic activity. Steel production, because of its role in many industries, is often thought to be a leading indicator. Car production and sales is a strong indicator of consumer spending but the figures tend to be volatile and influenced by other factors such as the availability of credit, launching of new models, etc.

None of these numbers is infallible and careful interpretation is needed. Confirmation of a trend in one statistic from a couple of others is a useful reality check. If business confidence is turning and steel production starts to revive, this might be proof that an upturn is on the way.

Employment and unemployment

Definition

Simple definitions are few and far between in labour market statistics. The first step is defining what we mean by the employed.

Employment numbers comprise the employed and the self-employed. The unemployment rate is normally calculated as people out of work (but ready and able to work) as a percentage of the total labour force. The labour force is usually reckoned to be the employed plus the unemployed.

It isn't quite as simple as that, though. Some statistics measure unemployment as being those out of work as a percentage of the 'economically active', while some count as unemployed only those actually claiming benefit.

Alternative names

'International Labour Organization (ILO) unemployment' (a standard international definition used for comparisons between countries) is substantially higher as a percentage than the 'claimant count', a strict measure of the percentage claiming unemployment benefit.

Economists generally divide unemployment into several different types. Some is seasonal (farming, hotels) and some is known as 'frictional', which refers to those temporarily between jobs. 'Structural' unemployment relates to the decline of once proud industries that employed large numbers (coal, steel, shipbuilding) as a result of technological change and international competition. Removing structural unemployment requires active measures to improve labour mobility and/or attract new industries to depressed areas.

The hard core of virtually unemployable people is known as 'residual' unemployment. Alternatively, figures sometimes quote the long-term unemployed (those unemployed for six months or more) as a percentage of the total unemployed as a figure for 'hard-core' unemployment.

In the US, there is less emphasis on unemployment and more stress on employment (or 'payroll') numbers. The non-farm payroll figures tend to be widely scrutinized because they have a direct bearing on consumer spending.

Unemployment concepts can be summarized in the following way:

- claimant = only those claiming benefit
- seasonal = those unemployed only at particular times of the year
- frictional = victims of redundancy and company failures
- structural = victims of major industrial decline
- residual = long-term jobless because of low skills/education.

How it's calculated

The range of definitions used for unemployment is a paradise for propagandists. At the time of writing, for example, the level of unemployed according to the ILO definition was 1.5m in the UK, whereas those actually claiming benefit were 951,000. Both figures are dwarfed by the figures for the economically inactive who are seeking a job: 2.24m.

The claimant count rate – the method most commonly used in the UK to measure unemployment – is the number of benefit claimants as a percentage of the number of claimants plus total workforce jobs.

Data for employment levels and unemployment in the UK is compiled in various ways, some of which involve sampling. Potential variations in the data as a result of sampling could be as much as 0.8% in the case of some statistics. They are generally put at less than half this.

Figures from the numbers of claimants and unfilled vacancies are calculated from administrative sources (JobCentre and Benefits Agency unemployment records) and so are considered to be pretty accurate. In the case of numbers for the total workforce jobs, the figures are derived from surveys of businesses and are subject to the usual caveats that surveys of this sort engender.

Employment and other labour market statistics in the US are calculated in much the same way as in the UK – from unemployment registers and survey data. Claimant unemployment is given less emphasis and allowance is made for the economically inactive – those who would work are classified as 'discouraged' workers.

These modest differences in terminology are nothing compared with those that exist internationally. There are many variations in the way unemployment is calculated in different countries. Germany, for example, excludes the self-employed from the labour force entirely. Even figures produced on standard ILO definitions suggest substantial variations between countries that strain credibility. The long-term unemployed as a percentage of total unemployed supposedly ranged from over 60% in Belgium, Italy and Austria to just 9% in the US.

Data is generally seasonally adjusted and subject to revision.

Recent changes

The UK produces voluminous statistics on the state of the labour market, with statistics that cover the national picture as well as statistics covering employment and unemployment trends in the region.

The figures are issued monthly, in the middle of the month, with most of the statistics around six weeks in arrears, with the exception of the claimant count rate, which covers the most recent completed month. Hence figures issued in mid-November would include the October claimant court but all other statistics would relate to periods up to the end of September.

Table 6.5 shows UK labour market statistics in early 2002.

Table 6.5 UK labour market statistics

Item	Period	Level (000s)	Rate (%)
Employment	Dec–Feb	28419	74.6
ILO unemployment	Dec–Feb	1520	5.1
Workforce jobs	Dec 01	29441	n/a
Claimant count	March 02	940	3.1

Source: National Statistics

Interpretation

The different definitions of unemployment figures do not in themselves make interpreting the numbers any more difficult. But you do need to make sure that you are comparing like with like when assessing newspaper comment on the subject or viewing the statistics.

It's also worth studying the precise wording when looking at press releases or newspaper articles. A figure that describes those 'looking for work' may be different from 'those claiming unemployment benefit'.

By the same token, absolute numbers of the unemployed are less meaningful than the rate itself (calculated on whatever definition is appropriate). Politicians have moved towards using claimant unemployment numbers. This is usually quoted using the term 'numbers out of work and claiming benefit'. Pedants might quarrel with this. A less tautological expression would be simply numbers claiming unemployment benefit. Those claiming benefit must by definition be out of work, at least officially. Claimant numbers do not include those who are out of work but not claiming benefit.

The claimant unemployment rate is used by the government as the yardstick for unemployment because it is appreciably lower than that calculated under the ILO formula. At the time of writing in the UK the two figures were two percentage points apart (5.1% versus 3.1%).

In both cases, however, what really matters is the trend, rather than the numbers or the rate. A rise in unemployment suggests an economy that is slowing down. It will have an adverse effect on consumer spending and consumer confidence.

As the number of self-employed individuals within the economy has increased, so the strict accuracy of the unemployment figures is harder to gauge. As a self-employed sole trader, I might not class myself as unemployed during a period when my workload is light. All it means is that I have time to dig the garden and take a few weeks holiday. Only if my livelihood shows signs of disappearing permanently am I likely to sign on as unemployed.

Unemployment figures are also broad numbers that balance out a number of conflicting trends within regions and sectors of the economy. Employment levels may be falling in Scotland, rising in the London area, falling in manufacturing and rising in service industries. Service businesses in the north-east may be seeing increases in employment, manufacturing businesses in the south-east may be seeing a decline.

It's also worth remembering that while they are invariably presented on a seasonally adjusted basis, there may be elements that are not stripped out of the figures (unseasonable weather and the influences of large-scale strikes are two examples).

Why is it important for you?

If you fear for your job, you are likely to be cautious about spending and borrowing, indeed about any form of economic activity. Rising unemployment, particularly in areas where there are limited alternative sources of employment, can have a chilling effect on the economy.

UK governments have striven in vain over the years to try to improve labour mobility, to encourage workers to retrain and to move to new areas where jobs are easier to find. Success has been limited.

The elimination of all unemployment is sometimes viewed as a political goal, but it would be a bad thing if it ever happened. An element of unemployment is to some degree a natural lubricant for economic activity, however hard it is to bear at the time (I speak as one who was unexpectedly made redundant at one stage in my career).

> The elimination of all unemployment is sometimes viewed as a political goal, but it would be a bad thing if it ever happened.

One phrase often used by economists is the non-accelerating inflation rate of unemployment, known by the acronym NAIRU. This is the minimum level to which unemployment can fall before further increases in demand, being unable to be accommodated by increased production of goods and services, result in higher inflation.

NAIRU is something of an elusive concept. It will vary from country to country and probably over time too as policies and attitudes change. Levels of minimum wages, average earnings, benefit rates, social attitudes and the age structure of the population are all likely to play a part in determining at exactly what point the fact that jobs are on offer and work is to be done will not tempt the unemployed or economically inactive back to work.

The other point is that unemployment figures arguably have more impact if they are rising. If you are in work, the fact that unemployment is falling is not of interest to you. It only assumes importance if you don't have a job. Similarly, if you're out of work, you will be indifferent to the fact that more people will be joining you, whereas those who are employed will experience some apprehension at the thought that their jobs and incomes are less secure than they were.

A final point is that employers typically adjust the level of the workforce at different speeds in different countries, depending on local custom and practice, the cost of laying off workers and legal constraints. In the US, for example, unemployment climbed exceptionally sharply after the September 11th 2001 terrorist attacks. On the other hand, the US has much greater labour mobility than many other countries and a considerably lower proportion of long-term unemployed than many European countries.

As a postscript it's worth recording that a number of other figures can be derived from the employment figures, including various measures of productivity (essentially productivity is GDP per employee, sometimes called output per filled job). Productivity is important because it is an element of economic growth. Economic growth reflects growth in demand, productivity and inflation. If productivity growth falters, economic growth will be that much less. At the time of writing, UK productivity had been running at a rate in the region of 2% but was slackening off sharply.

Figures for earnings are also contained in the employment report. We'll look at these in more detail in the next chapter.

IN BRIEF

- GDP measures the size of a country's economy.
- The GDP figures have their limitations due to what is **not** included, such as unpaid work and the 'black economy'.
- GDP growth and decline are good measures of economic performance and the only ones that can be compared internationally.
- Business confidence figures show the way the economy is moving before it is reflected in the official statistics.
- Industrial production statistics are of limited use to investors in general, but may be of use for workers and investors in particular industries.
- Unemployment figures are calculated in many ways and vary from country to country.
- The trend in unemployment is more important than the numbers. A rise suggests an economy is slowing down.

chapter seven

What we earn, save and borrow

Earnings, savings and borrowings are the counterpoint to the employment and unemployment statistics that we looked at in the previous chapter. They relate to what we earn and what we have left over to invest after our spending needs have been met.

In fact, it's fair to say that most economic statistics are related in some way. You may have deduced this already.

What we earn influences what we spend on consumption. Fear of unemployment may lead to a loss of confidence in our ability to maintain the lifestyle to which we've become accustomed. It can cause us to re-examine our lifestyle and perhaps put more into saving for a rainy day. If we save more and consume less, that itself can have an impact on the level of GDP and its growth rate.

If cheap borrowing is available and the cost of money is low, we may conclude that it's better to borrow now to buy assets we may not be able to afford in the future. If consumers are rational, however, they need to consider borrowing in the light of inflation too. Falling prices (deflation rather than inflation) make it more logical to postpone our spending – prices will be lower if we wait. Falling prices also mean that borrowing on fixed rates becomes a painful experience.

The problem, as we shall see later, is that consumers are anything but rational and logical. They often confuse nominal rates of interest with 'real' rates (i.e. those adjusted for inflation) and save for reasons other than the rate of interest on offer.

Interest rates are set only in part by the central bank. Central banks are not as all-powerful as is often supposed. In economies like the UK and US, the impact of securities and derivatives markets on the price of money is often equally important. They can be a better forecaster of likely changes in rates than scrutinizing the speeches of central bank bosses.

This chapter looks at these key measures of earnings, savings and borrowing: savings rates, the amount we save out of our incomes; average earnings, a general measure of remuneration including bonuses and overtime; and interest rates and how they are set.

Average earnings

Definition

Average earnings are figures for employee earnings, including bonuses and overtime payments. They are separate from wage rates. However, there is a great variety in the way the statistics are presented and you need to take extreme care when interpreting the numbers.

Alternative names

In the US, data on wages and other earnings is known as payroll data and presented along with employment numbers. In other parts of the world wages data has various names, including labour costs, wage rates and so on.

The central distinctions to draw are between wage rates, which describe basic pay per hour or per week, and earnings, which include bonuses and overtime. Earnings data can also be provided both before and after tax and other deductions such as national insurance in the UK or its equivalent in other countries. Earnings after deductions usually go under the phrase 'take-home pay'.

Some statistics also measure total employment costs. These include employers' contributions to pension schemes and on occasion payments in kind such as subsidized or free meals, company cars and the like.

How it's calculated

In the UK, government statisticians collect data on average earnings via a monthly wages and salaries survey. The results appear as an index number with a base date of 1995 = 100, and seasonally adjusted. The 'headline' rate is a three-month moving average that further smooths out the figures.

Each month's release provides an analysis of the figures, splitting out data for the private and public sector, and for manufacturing and services. The raw unadjusted figures are also given, and there is information on unit wage costs in manufacturing, that is, labour costs per unit of output. In this case the appropriate units of output will differ from respondent to respondent, so these figures are therefore presented as an index number. This means, of course, that there is an extra layer of statistical calculation involved in arriving at the figures. This may introduce further margins for error.

In the US, data on average hourly earnings and average weekly earnings is part of what is known as the Establishment Survey. It is also derived from other data, such as reported gross payrolls and the corresponding paid hours for workers in production and construction.

The US figures cover all workers apart from executive and professional in manufacturing industry and construction. They include all workers except for top management in service businesses. This is something of a mish-mash in definitional terms. No allowance is made for self-employed workers.

US payroll figures are compiled on the basis of a large survey of around 400,000 establishments. The figures are revised annually and the new, presumably more accurate, figures are incorporated into subsequent releases of the data.

Recent changes

As we saw in the last chapter, the UK produces voluminous statistics on the state of the labour market. There are statistics that cover the national picture as well as statistics covering employment and unemployment trends in the region. The figures also include data on average earnings and unit labour costs.

The figures are issued monthly, in the middle of the month, with most of the statistics showing the picture around six weeks in arrears. The exception to this is the claimant count rate, which covers the most recent completed month. This statistic was covered in the previous chapter. Earnings data issued in mid-November would include September provisional figures for average earnings. In the following month the provisional figure is revised.

Table 7.1 shows the average earnings in the UK for 2001.

Interpretation

The interplay between earnings, wage rates and employment gives something of a clue to the state of the economy.

The theory goes something like this. Average earnings, because they include overtime payments, tend to move ahead of wage rates as the economy recovers. Rather than take on extra staff if demand picks up, bosses will probably step up overtime for the existing workforce. Once the recovery seems more firmly established, they will take on additional workers and there may be upward pressure on wage rates.

> The interplay between earnings, wage rates and employment gives something of a clue to the state of the economy.

The same is true at the top of the cycle, when overtime rates and therefore average earnings begin to fall before wage rates do.

While this seems perfectly straightforward, in practice interpreting the statistics often isn't quite as simple. This is because there are several variables that go up to make average earnings.

Table 7.1 Statistics on UK average earnings

NSA 1995 = 100	Whole economy		Private sector		Public sector	
Month	Index	% ch	Index	% ch	Index	% ch
Jan 01	128.6	4.4	131.0	4.6	119.0	3.4
Feb 01	133.8	6.8	137.4	7.7	119.5	2.7
Mar 01	134.7	4.2	138.3	4.1	120.2	4.4
Apr 01	128.4	4.8	129.6	.4.6	123.4	5.7
May 01	127.6	4.3	128.7	4	123.6	5.6
Jun 01	129.2	4.8	130.4	4.6	124.5	5.5
Jul 01	128.8	4.2	129.7	3.7	125.1	6.6
Aug 01	127.8	4.4	128.4	3.9	125.4	6.3
Sep 01	127.6	4.4	128.4	4.1	124.5	5.8
Oct 01	128.1	4.4	129.1	1.1	124.3	5.7
Nov 01	128.6	3.7	129.7	3.5	124.2	4.8
Dec 01	134.1	2.1	136.0	1.5	126.4	5.1

Source: National Statistics

Wage rates can change, total hours worked can change, and there can be influences from profit sharing and bonus arrangements. These can distort the picture because they will inevitably be retrospective. They may affect the average earnings figure in one way, when the current underlying picture would actually suggest something different.

Changes in the mix of jobs, industrial disputes, regradings and promotions, and a range of other factors, can also influence the figures. In some instances these influences are gradual and may cancel each other out. There are also seasonal patterns that relate to the influence of the weather in industries where this is an important fact of life, such as construction. Seasonal adjustments allow for this to some degree, but unusually mild or cold conditions may make the numbers harder to interpret and make it hard to disentangle the underlying trends that the numbers may show. The timing of annual pay rounds can be hard to fit into the seasonal adjustment. In the US, for example, government employees generally get pay increases in January. Because these vary in size from year to year and come in the depths of winter, they distort the numbers.

Differences in definition between countries are rife. The most obvious additional drawback in most of them is that average earnings data largely ignores the self-employed sole-trader sector of the economy.

As a freelance writer, my revenue fluctuates unpredictably from month, to month with very little pattern from year to year. What I draw from the business as my 'wages' tends to vary to some degree with the cash flow available in the business. As more people have become self-employed, or have started up businesses where their main remuneration may be in the form of equity or stock options, so the accuracy of the earnings data becomes less.

Why is it important for you?

What we earn is important to all of us because it gives us spending power and saving power, as well as the ability to borrow.

Like unemployment figures, movements in average earnings are a bit like the phrase from the John Donne poem: 'Never send to know for whom the bell tolls: it tolls for thee.'

We can, as individuals, be sure that if unemployment is rising there is a chance that our own jobs may be on the line before long. Similarly, if average earnings come under pressure, it's a sign that our own overtime might be cut and that we had better rein in our spending in preparation for tougher times. If we do so, it's likely that our personal savings ratio will rise. Savings are covered in the next section.

Savings ratio

Definition

The savings ratio is the percentage that savings represent of total personal disposable income. In other words it is what is left over out of our incomes after all forms of taxes and spending have been taken out.

Alternative names

The savings ratio is sometimes known as the savings rate or personal savings. National savings measure all form of saving, whether personal, corporate or government. Government saving takes the form of budget surpluses, corporate saving is surplus or 'free' cash flow after tax, dividends and sufficient capital spending to maintain a company's assets. Much of the press comment on saving relates solely to personal saving and savings rates and ignores the business and public sector dimension.

How it's calculated

There are several factors that make personal savings a hard statistic to calculate with any degree of precision. In the first place there is no specific way to calculate it 'from the ground up' from survey data. The reason is that many individuals would simply (for reasons of privacy) refuse to divulge exactly what their savings were and how they fluctuated.

As a result the savings ratio ends up being calculated as a residual from the GDP and consumer spending statistics. It's what's left over after taxes and spending have been deducted. Figures arrived at in this way are often highly volatile. This is because small changes in other variables can produce a big percentage change in the much smaller residual number. Nonetheless market commentators pay attention to the savings rate. It is usually expressed as a percentage and is monitored for changes over fairly lengthy time periods.

Recent changes

Data on savings levels and savings ratios in the UK between 1999 and 2001 is shown in Table 7.2. This is derived quarterly from GDP data and revised frequently.

Interpretation

Interpreting changes in savings ratios is hard. In the US, for example, the whole issue of saving has become closely bound up with the value of investment portfolios, the level of the stock market, the level of house prices, and the ease with which mortgages can be refinanced to transfer home equity into personal bank accounts.

The whole phenomenon goes by the name of the 'wealth effect'. In other words, when share prices are rising, individuals tend to save little and even consume savings by spending the profits from share transactions. Lower interest rates also lead many consumers to refinance their mortgages to take advantage of lower rates and free up cash for additional spending. By contrast, if house prices drop and if the stock market falls, precautionary saving should increase – although it is hard to credit it in the gung-ho consumer society in America.

By common consent savings rates in the US have declined steadily in the last decade and have been close to zero for some time. This contrasts sharply with the position in some other countries, where frugality is an article of faith for the population. In France and Japan, for example, savings rates are as much as 14% of disposable income. In the UK, the figure is the 4–6% area.

Table 7.2 Statistics on UK household savings

Gross household income and expenditure (seasonally adjusted)				
		Income	Savings	Savings ratio (%)
1999	Q1	144668	4235	2.8
	Q2	153397	11072	7.0
	Q3	150957	6367	4.1
	Q4	155521	8060	5.1
2000	Q1	154582	5649	3.6
	Q2	157716	7221	4.5
	Q3	158564	6778	4.2
	Q4	162251	7286	4.4
2001	Q1	166245	10812	6.4
	Q2	167654	10225	5.9
	Q3	170969	9277	5.3
	Q4	171650	9126	5.2
% change:				
on prior quarter		0.4		
on same quarter of prior year		6.3		

Source: National Statistics

Only in Sweden and the Netherlands, where taxes are high and social provision of welfare benefits exceptional, are savings rates anywhere near as low as they are in the US.

One should beware of placing too much reliance on these figures, though. International comparisons fall foul of the different definitions of saving used in various countries and of differences as simple as the types of credit products available in different economies and how savings and investment income are taxed.

Should the purchase of a car be treated as consumption or investment? Is putting money into a pension fund an outlay or an element of saving? Ditto life assurance? And how should interest payments and depreciation be treated? According to *The Economist*, differences in definition alone account for three percentage points of the difference in the savings ratio between the US and Japan.

There are several other factors that affect saving. One important one is the age structure of the population. The elderly save less than the thirty-somethings. The elderly have low incomes but consume savings and investments made earlier by reducing their capital and buying annuities from accumulated pension savings. The thirtysomethings are approaching peak earning power, the point where they begin to save enthusiastically for retirement (or should do).

This is one reason for muting one's optimism about stock market trends in the next decade or so. In contrast to the 1980s, for example, when the post-war baby boom was at its peak earning and therefore saving power, the period from 2005 onwards will be one where the retired baby boomers – people like me, in fact – are consuming their savings rather than investing them.

Why is it important for you?

Surprising though it might seem given the emphasis placed on interest rates in the press, consumers have often not acted logically when it comes to saving. There are several factors governing saving and borrowing that pull in opposite directions.

Ostensibly consumers should borrow when inflation is high, since the rise in prices will erode the burden of the debt over time. Conversely, they should save (i.e. avoid debt) when inflation is low, for the opposite reason.

Borrowing when prices are rising only slowly, or possibly likely to fall, does not make sense. In the 1970s, however, high levels of saving accompanied high inflation rates, a fact which is explained by the parlous economic situation at the time. Similarly, savings were low in the US in the 1990s, explained partly by the wealth effect (described earlier) of a high and rising stock market. Since it was consumption that has bolstered the US economy, now times have turned more difficult there have been fears that an increase in precautionary saving could reignite a recession.

In reality personal savings are the result of a complex mix of factors, but consumers rarely save for logical reasons. They tend to save for peace of mind, and when nominal rates of interest are high. They tend not to save as much when real rates of interest suggest they should or when inflation is low.

It's also worth noting that at the same time as consumers have been gearing up their personal balance sheets and reducing savings, companies have been doing the same, again most notably in the US, by issuing debt to buy in shares.

According to a tenet of financial theory that I have personally never subscribed to, investors should be indifferent to how a company is financed. In practice – and as many examples demonstrate – confidence is all and, especially when times are tough, investors shy away from companies with high levels of debt. The extent to which companies accumulate cash or take on debt is the counterpart to consumers' saving and dis-saving.

Nonetheless, just as consumers in the US and elsewhere have taken on more debt, so companies have followed exactly the same path.

One final point about saving and interest rates is another element of illogic. It is that consumers rarely act logically when it comes to assessing the relative cost of different forms of debt. The boom in credit card debt, which, though actively marketed, is an extremely expensive form of borrowing if the consumer has access to other sources of finance, is a modern phenomenon. It speaks volumes for the lack of an educated appreciation of the real financial facts of life. Many consumers take the credit that is most freely offered to them, without examining its cost or looking for cheaper alternatives.

In short, the choice of debt – if you happen to be hooked on it – is more determined by the availability of supply rather than necessarily its price. The borrowing addict will pay whatever rate it takes to get a line of credit.

Interest rates

This section takes a slightly different format to the rest of the book because interest rates are slightly different to other economic statistics. Rather than being compiled by statisticians, they are available in the market on a daily basis and are therefore readily apparent and unambiguous. We don't need to agonize about how they are calculated or whether they are accurate.

Why rates matter

Interest rates are the cost of money. And since modern economies float on a pool of credit, the level of interest rates affects the level of economic activity. Cheaper money, in the form of lower interest rates, will stimulate economic activity (other things being equal) and dearer money (higher interest rates) will restrict economic activity.

In most advanced industrial countries the central bank sets the level of interest rates. In the US this is the Federal Reserve, in the Euro-zone the ECB, and in the UK the Bank of England. But in setting the base level of borrowing rates, central banks have to reconcile a number of conflicting objectives. One is to regulate the speed at which the economy is growing.

Central banks raise interest rates to make it more expensive for businesses and financial institutions to expand. This restricts activity and cools the economy, and slows down inflation. Similarly, lowering rates is an economic stimulus, but one that is not without external consequences.

Lower interest rates in the UK make the pound sterling a less attractive currency in which investors might hold surplus balances. So a cut in interest rates might mean a lower value for the pound on the foreign exchanges.

This is also a stimulus in one sense, since it makes our exports cheaper. But it also makes imports, for which we have a particular addiction, more expensive, importing inflation and worsening the trade balance. We'll look at this in more detail in the next chapter.

Different types of rate: the terminology

There are several puzzling terms often used when commentators talk about interest rates. Let's go through a few of them.

Repo rates: Bank rate and minimum lending rate are old-fashioned terms now in the market. The Bank of England, ECB and the Federal Reserve, when they wish to change interest rates, adjust what is known as the repo rate.

Repos, or repurchase agreements, are collateralized loans (backed by cash or high-quality short-term government debt) used by traders in the financial markets to finance and gear up their trading books. The central bank can set the rate charged for loans and borrowing it undertakes in this way for its own account. This is an indirect means of controlling the overall cost and supply of money.

Discount rates: These are slightly different. These are the rates at which the central bank will provide the banking system with money over a slightly longer time period than just a few hours.

LIBOR: There are other rates that are often used in market commentary. One is LIBOR (London Inter Bank Offered Rate). This is the rate that banks will lend money to other banks in the system and is a key, market-determined, short-term interest rate. Most other countries have an equivalent. For the Euro-zone the rate is called EURIBOR (Euro Inter Bank Offered Rate).

Fed Funds: In the US the Federal Funds rate is the rate at which commercial banks receive or pay interest on funds they deposit in the central banking system or draw from it. This is a sensitive indicator of the supply and demand for money because, unlike the discount rate, the market sets it on a daily basis.

In all markets the official repo rate is changed only periodically when a central bank wants to highlight a big, set-piece change in the level of interest rates.

Bank base rates: Although in the UK the minimum lending rate used to be called the base rate, this now has a different meaning. This is the rate on which the commercial banks will base the interest rate they charge on loans or pay on deposits. In the case of loans a variable amount will be added to the base rate to reflect the perceived status of the buyer as a 'good risk' or not. Blue-chip companies might pay half a percentage point over base rate while the man in the street pays two or three percentage over the odds because he or she is judged less likely to be good for the money.

Base lending rates also ultimately determine the price of other forms of credit, from car loans and various forms of consumer credit, rates on credit cards, and mortgage rates. The base rate is not the only factor in play in the way in which these rates are set. The degree to which the loan is secured and the quality of the borrower are others.

Within the mortgage market, for example, those borrowing on a fixed rate can expect to pay a higher rate than someone whose mortgage payments are tied to base rates and may float up and down accordingly. Mortgages with capped rates will cost more than a floating rate mortgage and may have penalties for early redemption. What sort of rate you pay and how much you can borrow will depend on how the bank perceives you as a credit risk. If you are self-employed or considered a bad credit risk, you will pay more.

> If you are self-employed or considered a bad credit risk, you will pay more.

However, the days when the banks had complete control over the supply of credit in the economy, and building societies dominated the mortgage market, have long gone. The rise of the bond markets and tradable securities that are tantamount to bank loans has eaten into the lending banks' ability to call the shots on the interest rate scene.

Commercial paper: Commercial paper, for example, represents one way in which companies can raise money from investors without necessarily having recourse to a bank. Commercial paper takes the form of short-term IOUs issued by companies and traded in the market at interest rates set by the market in the form of a discount to the paper's face value on maturity.

Interest rate futures: In addition, futures markets provide an indication of the level of short-term interest rates. Short-term interest rate futures typically trade at a discount that represents the expected interest rate at the time the future expires. Hence if it is now December and the February short sterling interest rate future is trading at 97, this means that dealers are expecting the official short-term rate to be at 3% when the future expires in mid-February. Futures are also traded on the EURIBOR rate.

Futures prices can be used to estimate the probability of a change in rates over the period in question. The closer the futures price to a particular level, the higher the probability. If rates are currently 3.5% and the futures price for February delivery is 96.9, this could be taken as an 80% likelihood that the rate will be at 3% by February.

Bond markets and interest rates

Bond yields are also interest rates in disguise. UK and US government bonds have never defaulted, either in terms of paying interest in full and on time or in repaying capital at maturity in full and on time. So investors regard them as risk-free.

What investors are prepared to pay for bonds and therefore what they will receive by way of a return reflects in part the preference for being paid sooner rather than later (normally long-term bond yields have to be higher than short-term ones) and investors' views of economic growth and inflation. We'll look at this in a bit more detail later.

In a way, though, what's important for the markets is not necessarily what might be important for you and me. The markets will anticipate rate changes and look at trends in interest rates and how they interact with economic activity. If you or I go to the bank or to another credit provider for a loan, what will govern our ability to borrow is not so much the rate as the availability of credit and whether or not we are considered a good risk.

In the same way, companies perceived to be in financial difficulty will find it more costly to borrow, whether from a bank or through the securities market. Bond investors will demand a bigger premium in the yield on the bond over and above the risk-free rate on a government bond repaid at the same time.

Banks do not have to lend to financially unsound companies. Accounting problems at companies, or simple loss of confidence, often result in bankruptcies, simply because the companies concerned have no avenue to turn to. Borrowing in the markets is too costly, and banks will not lend. The company goes bust because it simply runs out of cash.

Yield curves

Understanding the way a yield curve works is the key to understanding the significance of interest rates and the economy.

While futures prices indicate where the market sees short-term interest rates settling in a month or two's time, the influence of the yield curve is more fundamental. The previous book in this series, *First Steps in Bonds*, covers this topic in more detail, but here is a brief flavour of it.

The yield curve is a visual representation of the way yields vary according to the maturity dates of the bonds in question. Because of the preference of most investors for liquidity, yields on longer-dated bonds are typically higher than those on very short-term ones. It's a version of the same phenomenon that means that your instant-access account earns a lower rate of interest than one where you have to give 90-day notice of withdrawal.

Because yields in government bond markets reflect supply and demand and investor expectations of what may happen, the theoretical curve that should slope up smoothly from left to right might not always materialize. A curve that slopes the opposite way is known as an inverted yield curve. This is where short-term yields are higher than long-term ones. It is far from rare, but it doesn't often offer clear signals to the market.

The inversion in the UK yield curve which began in October 1998 and ended in the course of 2001 may have been caused initially by the demand from pension funds for longer-dated gilts in the wake of the imposition of new rules governing pension fund investment.

Investors often assume that a flattening of the yield curve will normally be accomplished by a sharp fall in short-term interest rates as set by the Bank of England, and hence a reduction in short-dated gilt-edge yields. But this is not always the case. The curve could flatten because long-term yields increase.

The ability of pundits to forecast market movements on the basis of the yield curve has also been disproved by recent events.

The conventional wisdom is that once the inversion of the yield curve has happened, share prices will start to improve. Short-term rates will be cut, boosting prices of short-dated gilts. And because rates have been cut, the economy will expand, boosting company profits and share prices. However, this is not always the case and it is far from obvious whether there is any direct cause and effect.

This theory has worked on three out of the five occasions since the early 1980s when an inverted yield curve has been seen. Bond prices rose, but shares rose more, in the period between March 1980 and June 1981, between September 1981 and May 1982, and between February 1985 and May 1987.

In the long period of recession from October 1989 to August 1992, just before Britain was forced from the Exchange Rate Mechanism (ERM), returns from equities were meagre and gilts showed double-figure annual returns.

There are those who claim that the same may be true this time round. In particular, low interest rates do not necessarily result in economic expansion – as the example of Japan in the 1990s makes clear – if there are other drags on economic activity, such as financial problems at major companies, excess capacity, high unemployment and lack of confidence.

That said, and for good or ill, the spread (difference in yield) between very short-term rates and the benchmark ten-year government bond is generally regarded as a leading indicator. If the spread is positive and increasing (long-term bonds increasingly yield more than short-term ones), it indicates a steeper yield curve. This is better than a low spread that pays investors little premium for investing long term.

One reason why interest rates may not have worked as well of late at providing economic stimulus in the US is because to some degree consumers have funded additional spending by refinancing their mortgages. Mortgage refinancing in America is, however, based on longer-term bond yields rather than short-term interest rates. And bond yields stayed stubbornly high despite sharp cuts in short-term rates.

One reason for this is tied up with the way the bond markets act as predictive tools in other ways. Because the income from them is fixed, all conventional government bonds are particularly sensitive to the prospects for inflation. If inflation, which is the sworn enemy of bondholders, looks like rising, bond prices will fall and yields will rise to compensate for the greater risk of capital erosion in real terms over the life of the bond. It may be that investors currently feel that a recovering economy will stoke inflation.

Switching this idea on its head and basing the assumption on the fact that the market often anticipates events, falling long-term bond prices are often interpreted as a sign that inflation may be about to pick up.

Either way, observing the movement in interest rates and bond yields in the market – in other words the elements of interest rates that are not set by central banks – can tell us a lot about where the economy is headed.

How interest rates are set

In recent years there has been a concerted move for central banks in the US and Europe to make the decision-making process surrounding the setting of interest rates more transparent. Hence the tendency has been for central banks to establish policy committees that attempt to reach a consensus on what needs to be done, and whose deliberations are made public at a later date so that observers can get clues as to how rates might move at a later meeting.

Meeting dates are scheduled in advance, although occasionally the central bank governor may make an inter-meeting adjustment to rates if the situation warrants it, as was the case, for example, in the wake of the 11 September terrorist attacks in 2001.

Much analysis and comment is made on the movements of the Fed, the ECB and the Bank of England. In the UK, for example, the Monetary Policy Committee minutes are scrutinized for signs of disagreement among the members. In reality, however, investors need only look to the futures market to discern exactly where the market at any one time expects interest rates to stand.

As alluded to previously, one big problem that policymakers face is that the interest rates have an uncertain effect on an economy. Interest rate reductions take time to work through the system and the degree to which they exert a stimulus depends from market to market. In the US, for example, consumers are able to refinance their mortgages quickly and easily and thus adjust their payments, but usually only in line with medium and long-term bond yields, not short-term interest rates.

In the UK, where for many floating rate mortgages are the norm and home-ownership is a national pastime, the impact of rate cuts is more direct.

One particular problem in the US is that the whole issue of interest rates has become inextricably linked with the stock market. Interest rate cuts are seen, perhaps mistakenly, as evidence that the Federal Reserve doesn't want the stock market bubble to deflate. Hence consumers have become over confident in their spending, which makes the potential damage from a collapse in confidence that much greater.

At the same time, if confidence does collapse because the credit bubble has become unsustainable, there is a limit to the extent to which further rate cuts will apply a stimulus. Rates cannot be cut below zero. If the economy is lethargic with rates at very low levels, there is little more that policymakers can do to apply stimulus, at least in terms of monetary action.

Interest rate statistics

Definition

Interest rates are the cost of borrowing or the return for lending money. This can be either in the form of a loan or its equivalent in the securities market, such as bond or certificate of deposit. As explained in the previous section, a variety of interest rate data is available. Interest rates are set by reference to a basic underlying rate determined by the central bank. All other rates tend to be derived from this.

Alternative names

Different interest rates have different names and different countries use different technology. (See the previous section for a summary of what these various rates mean.)

How it's calculated

The Bank of England publishes interest rate statistics in the UK on a monthly basis. The data typically appears as a time series of monthly averages, weighted in importance by the volume of borrowing and lending at that particular rate on a particular day. The statistics are generally released for one month towards the end of the following month.

Rate information is given on banks' lending to a range of customer sectors of differing credit quality – the public sector, building societies, companies, households – and in different forms. These different forms include rates on demand deposits, deposits that require notice, mortgage lending, credit card debt and so on.

Statistics are also provided giving yields on government securities of various maturities, and of short-term rates for money lent to and borrowed from the banking system on a 'wholesale' basis. These include repo rates, discount rates, LIBOR, SONIA (Sterling Over Night Index Average) and so on.

In the US, the Federal Reserve issues statistics on interest rates on a daily, weekly and monthly basis. These are rates for the full range of interest rate products including Fed funds, commercial paper, CDs, the discount rate, US Treasury bills, notes and bonds, corporate bonds and so on.

The ECB also issues statistics for the Euro area as a whole, EU countries outside the Euro-zone (including Britain) and for individual EU members' national markets. Statistics are presented primarily in graphical form and relate to interest rates at the 'retail' level (i.e. for borrowing and lending by private individuals).

Recent changes

Table 7.3 gives some brief data on changes in interest rates in the UK between 1999 and the first quarter of 2002.

Interpretation

The preceding section described the rates set by central bank policymakers and those determined by the interaction of supply and demand in the market.

Investors need to look at several aspects of the ways rates are derived. They need to look at the shape of the yield curve, the thoughts of central bank policymakers as expressed in their official utterances, and bond yields and interest rate futures prices to come to a judgement as to how interest rate movements might affect the economy.

It is worth remembering that interest rate policy is permissive. Low interest rates will permit a greater level of economic expansion to take place, but consumers and businesses don't have to follow the interest rate lead. The impact of interest rate policy can be blunted by structural factors, such as the flexibility (or lack of it) of mortgage finance, and by confidence issues related to the level of unemployment, the price of shares, international political developments and a range of other factors.

Why is it important for you?

Interest rates affect us all, as savers, borrowers and consumers. Not everyone wants interest rates to be low. Those who rely on investment income to keep body and soul together tend to prefer rates to be higher than they often are.

This is worth recalling when watching pundits discuss interest rates – the discussion generally focuses around the beneficial effect of lower interest rates. But there is a sizeable section of the population – pensioners and others on fixed incomes – that doesn't see it quite that way.

Table 7.3 Selected UK interest rate statistics

End-quarter rates (%)		SONIA	SIBR 3mo	Euro$ 3mo	B of E Repo	3mo£Tbill
1999	Q4	3.04	5.97	6.03	6.00	5.62
2000	Q1	5.72	6.19	6.32	5.75	5.84
	Q2	5.26	6.14	6.79	5.50	5.85
	Q3	6.18	6.11	6.77	5.25	5.76
	Q4	4.36	5.83	6.41	5.00	5.61
2001	Q1	6.05	5.45	4.92	4.75	5.22
	Q2	4.71	5.22	3.85	4.50	5.04
	Q3	5.17	4.44	2.57	4.00	4.28
	Q4	4.95	4.05	1.86	4.00	3.83
2002	Q1	3.27	4.13	2.05	4.00	4.00

Source: Bank of England

IN BRIEF

- Earnings, wage rates and employment figures all play a part in determining the state of the economy.

- Calculating personal savings statistics is difficult, relying as it does on the disclosure of personal information, which may not be forthcoming.

- The definition of 'savings' varies from country to country.

- Consumers should borrow when inflation is high and save when it is low, but often do the opposite.

- The level of interest rates affects the level of economic activity.

- For companies *and* individuals, the smaller the risk, the cheaper the borrowing.

- Yield curves measure returns available on bonds of successively longer repayment periods. An inverted yield curve (short-term returns higher than long-term ones) signals impending recession.

- Low interest rates are preferred by businesses but not by those relying on a fixed return from savings and investments.

chapter eight

How we trade

Foreign trade has always been important for the British economy. Those with long memories will recall the balance of payments crises of the 1960s and 1970s. Poor economic management caused them. Imports exceeded exports, foreign confidence in the pound was low, and because there was a commitment to maintain a fixed value for the pound, reserves were depleted as the financial markets sold pounds in exchange for dollars from the Bank of England's reserves.

Eventually, in circumstances like this, the government had to throw in the towel and devalue the currency, to the accompaniment of exhortations to voters that the 'pound in their pocket' had not been devalued. Unless that is, they wanted to travel abroad or buy an imported product. There was an echo of this when Britain was forced out of the ERM in 1992.

Britain has always been a trading nation, so statistics on imports and exports have long been seen as a crucial part of the economic picture. Britain now exports services more than it exports manufactured goods. Shipping, insurance, and the trading and advisory work that goes on in the City are unseen exports that are bought by governments, companies and individuals in other countries – in other words, 'invisible' exports.

Only the uniquely British sense of humour of a Whitehall civil servant could invent the name of the organization that used to be concerned with promoting this aspect of the economy – 'British Invisibles'.

> Britain has always been a trading nation, so statistics on imports and exports have long been seen as a crucial part of the economic picture.

The important indicator of the health of the British economy as far as trade with the rest of the world is concerned is the relatively simple notion of the balance of trade. This is the difference between imports and exports: in crude terms, the foreign trade 'current account'.

The capital account, which ought to measure the degree to which foreigners are investing in the economy on a long-term basis, in fact reflects the impact of more speculative flows of capital, which dominate the figures. The capital account is important, but arguably less so than in the past because Britain is not committed to maintaining a particular exchange rate value for the pound. We don't want to see volatility in the rate, but modest fluctuations – even if caused by so-called 'hot money' – can be managed and viewed with relative equanimity.

Nonetheless the balance of payments, the collective name for all this, works according to strict double-entry bookkeeping principles. For every credit there is a debit, both current account and capital account must agree, and the balance must be zero. Commentators tend to focus, rightly of course, on where the imbalances occur and how they change.

For other economies, particularly those of developing countries, commodity prices assume considerable importance. The interplay between exchange rates, commodity prices and foreign trade gives rise to a concept known as the terms of trade, which at its crudest simply expresses the relative movement in the prices of exports and imports.

For many countries this is crucial to how quickly they can develop. Their growth prospects have been hindered because they are forced to import from hard currency countries, while their revenues from the sale of natural resources have been adversely affected by slumping prices on world commodity markets.

Commodity prices themselves play an interesting role in economic forecasting. Because there is a natural demand for certain commodities in many industrial processes, the prices of some commodities (copper is a good example) often turn up when economic activity improves. Watching futures prices for these commodities can give a clue to turning points in the economy.

Lest we dismiss all this as remote from our daily lives, it's worth reflecting that the spread of globalization means that the foreign trade statistics are important to us all. This is not just because we may unknowingly buy something that is made in a sweatshop in China but sold to us through a retailer owned by a US company. It is also because if Britain, or any other country, is an attractive destination for foreign investors, it may result in new factories being built and jobs being created. With this in mind, let's have a look at some of these indicators.

Foreign trade and the balance of payments

Definition

Trade and balance of payments statistics can be rich seams of misunderstanding and sloppy use of terminology. The balance of payments is a generic term for sets of interlocking transactions and balances, of which trade in goods and services is only a part.

It has several component parts: visible trade (i.e. importing and exporting physical goods); invisibles (trade in services); the balance of transfers of rent, interest profit and dividends into and out of the country (often abbreviated to RIPD); net transfers by individuals which might, for example, include remittances made to relatives abroad by foreigners working in this country or into this country by British citizens working abroad. Adding all these balances together gets you to the current account balance.

In other words the current account balance is the difference between the value of what we buy from and sell abroad, either in the form of goods or services, and what individuals send or receive from abroad. It also includes the returns received on capital invested abroad by us or paid out on capital invested domestically by foreigners.

The capital account moves on from this and takes into account the balance of direct investment (i.e. factories that foreigners may have built in this country minus we may have built abroad), the balance of portfolio investment (shares and bonds bought by UK investors abroad less UK investments bought by foreigners), and the net effect of short-term speculative movements of capital into and out of the economy, sometimes called 'hot money'.

To summarize:

- Current account balance = visible trade balance + invisibles balance + RIPD.

- Capital account = net direct investment + net portfolio investment + 'hot money'.

- Surplus (or shortfall) = addition to (or subtraction from) foreign currency reserves.

Hedge fund managers and professional currency traders are the prime conduits for hot money and can make or break currencies (though they usually deny it) and disrupt trade and economic activity generally. Their interventions are usually made (or supposedly justified) on the grounds that their actions force governments to face up to economic reality – or at least their version of it.

The balance of all these current and capital flows has to be met by changes in official reserves and balances at the IMF, giving an overall balance equal to zero.

Alternative names

It's easy to summarize this, and the various names involved:

- Current account:
  - Exports minus imports of goods = balance of visible trade.
  - Exports minus imports of goods and services = balance of trade in goods and services.
  - As above + balance of other current transfers = current account balance.

■ Capital account:
- Current account balance + net direct investment = the 'core' balance.
- Core balance + net long-term portfolio movements = the 'basic' balance.
- Basic balance plus speculative capital flows = net official financing requirement.

When reading press reports on the balance of payments it is worth bearing these distinctions in mind. Journalists are apt to play fast and loose with the terminology. We need to keep in mind exactly which part of the trade 'balance sheet' is being discussed.

How it's calculated

Statistics relating to trade in goods and services and the balance of payments should be easy to compile. Trade, whether in the form of physical goods, services or capital, invariably involves some form of documentation – bills of lading, letters of credit, import duties and so on – which can be sampled to arrive at the figures.

Trade statistics come from two official sources. UK Trade Statistics measure the goods and services component of the equation and are the ones that have a bearing on domestic economic activity. Balance of payments statistics include the capital account and focus on flows of money rather than physical movement or changes of ownership. In other words, a UK investor investing abroad will show up as an outflow from the UK, even though he may still own the, now foreign, asset.

There are other technical differences in measurement that mean that the value of imports or exports recorded on one set of statistics may not match those recorded in the other. Balance of payments figures for exports and imports should match those in the GDP and national income statistics.

Recent changes

Trade statistics take time to compile. Figures for trade with the world normally appear about six weeks after the end of the month in question, but those for trade in goods with non-EU countries are produced more quickly and released at the same time. Hence, world trade figures issued in mid-December would cover the period to end-October but would be accompanied by non-EU trade in goods for November. Table 8.1 shows statistics for the UK balance of trade for 2001.

In the US, the statistics are compiled in much the same way from official documentation and take about the same length of time to compile.

Table 8.1 Statistics on UK balance of trade

All figures in £bn and seasonally adjusted

| 2001 | Balance of trade in goods | | | Balance of trade in services (invisibles) | Total balance |
	EU	Non-EU	World		
May	-0.4	-2.4	-2.9	1.4	-1.5
June	-0.4	-3.0	-3.4	1.4	-2.0
July	-0.1	-2.4	-2.5	1.2	-1.2
August	-0.3	-2.9	-3.3	1.0	-2.0
September	-0.5	-1.8	-2.3	0.3	-1.9
October	-0.6	-1.7	-2.3	0.9	-1.4
November	-0.8	-2.1	-2.8	1.1	-1.8
December	-0.8	-2.4	-3.2	1.1	-2.1

Note: Figures may not add up due to rounding.

Source: National Statistics

Interpretation

We need to be careful of paying too much attention to figures like this. While they indicate broad trends, there have been examples of very large items being missed out of the figures for several years, eventually turning up because some eagle-eyed statisticians checked an old file.

It's also worth remembering that official statistics do not measure illicit trade. In the UK's case, this includes not just drugs and other organized crime activity, but also smuggling of tobacco and alcohol across the Channel because of duty disparities between France and Britain. In some countries the scale of the black economy means that trade statistics can be seriously flawed.

Even in legitimate trade there are leads and lags between payments and receipts. Hence reading too much into one month's figures can be dangerous. The figures may be distorted simply because a large shipment of high-value goods was delivered in one month but paid for in the next. Deliveries and payments of ships and aircraft, for example, have typically had a significant effect on the numbers.

> On a global scale, foreign trade statistics show the world importing significantly more than it exports. Clearly this cannot be so.

As several observers have also recorded, the figures simply don't add up. Statisticians make the figures balance with a so-called balancing item, but this doesn't entirely solve the problem.

On a global scale, foreign trade statistics show the world importing significantly more than it exports. Clearly this cannot be so. Either imports are being double-counted, or exports are going unrecorded for some reason. The fact that inaccuracies like this crop up to some degree leads to scepticism about the trade figures as a whole.

Why is it important for you?

There's a temptation to think that none of this matters unduly, but even in an era of floating exchange rates, where it is the currency that takes the strain of speculative capital flows rather than currency reserves, the numbers do have significance.

They matter not least because of precisely this foreign exchange dimension: they do affect the currency and hence often have a knock-on effect to domestic interest rate policy. If imports surge, this will often be accompanied by weakness in the currency, if only because dollars (or pounds) will have to be sold and foreign currency bought to pay for them.

Higher imports and a falling value of the currency may result in interest rates being raised to stem a further fall. A fall in the value of the currency increases domestic inflation because imported goods become more expensive.

The reverse is also true. Strong export performance by the US, for example, would bid up the price of the dollar, cheapen imports and lower interest rates.

The US has often run large deficits on its trade balance. It is able to do this with a certain amount of impunity because of the dollar's position as a universally accepted benchmark currency. In times of crisis, the dollar is seen as a safe haven and historically America's reputation for a robust economy has added to the dollar's attraction. This has meant that the US is a natural home for savings from investors around the world. It will remain so while investors have confidence in the robustness of the US economy.

The result is that rates can be kept lower and imports financed more easily than if this were not the case. But if the world ever loses confidence in America's currency, perhaps because an equally robust currency and economy emerges, the adjustment process could be painful.

It is for this reason perhaps that many economists in the US are paying particular attention to the way European economic integration is proceeding and to the strength or otherwise of the Euro, especially since it has become a tangible reality to travellers and the man in the street.

It also neatly illustrates the point that it is what happens in currency markets, the barometer of international flows of capital, which is sometimes a more important facet of the trade picture than the actual physical movement of goods and services.

This is not to say that a trade deficit doesn't occasionally spook the market. The stock market crash of 1987 was brought about in part because of nervousness over the trade and budget deficits in the US. It was quietly forgotten, but the same degree of nervousness can easily be generated in the future, for as long as American consumers continue to live beyond their means by spending what are in effect the savings of foreigners.

Exchange rates

Definition

Exchange rates are simply the market price of one currency expressed in terms of another. The rate is the number of units of one currency that a single unit of the other will buy. A £/US dollar exchange rate stated as $1.43 means that £1 will buy $1.43, £10 will buy $14.30 and so on.

Exchange rates link any major currency with any other. Some rates are more important than others because they have greater significance in terms of world trade and financial transactions. Hence news reports tend to concentrate on rates that involve the pound, the US dollar, the Euro and the Japanese yen.

Alternative names

Exchange rates are sometimes called by a range of other names. Dealers often call the sterling/dollar rate 'cable'. The reason for this dates back to the 1930s when most international currency remittances involved the sterling/dollar rate and the money was telegraphed (or cabled) to the recipient. Hence the international value of sterling and the word 'cable' became synonymous. More prosaically, exchange rates are also sometimes known as cross rates or currency pairs.

The exchange rate for immediate settlement is universally known as the spot rate. However, currency markets also have a full range of sophisticated derivative instruments. Hence one can buy and sell currency futures and options, or buy and sell currency for forward delivery. Certain derivatives exchanges have specialized in futures and options in currencies.

Companies often buy currencies forward in order to minimize the risks they run in having unavoidable currency exposure through export sales and overseas subsidiaries or to have predictability in the interest payments they must make on their foreign currency borrowings.

Forward rates and currency futures normally move exactly in line with the spot rate and have no predictive value. This contrasts with interest rate futures, to which are frequently ascribed predictive properties.

How it's calculated

Currency rates reflect the pull of supply and demand in the markets.

Foreign exchange markets are among the most liquid, but it is worth bearing in mind that they are some way from being the perfect markets of economic theory. They satisfy some of the conditions of perfect competition – a large crowd of buyers and sellers, for example, and a free flow of information. They do not, however, simply reflect transactions needed to facilitate world trade, but are in addition a speculative medium.

Large, well-funded speculators and traders buy and sell currencies on the basis of the full gamut of emotions that are rife in the market – fear and greed, hope, political calculation, technical analysis and a range of other reasons. These may reflect economic and political realities, or they may simply reflect the emotions of the crowd.

Governments also intervene periodically in the market, sometimes in an attempt to wrong-foot traders and to stabilize what they may see as an unwarranted movement in their currency in one direction or another.

In broad terms, though, and certainly over time, a currency's strength or weakness should reflect its underlying economic performance and the favour with which it is viewed by the international financial community. Speculators are merely trying to make it reach its 'correct' value quicker.

A better measure of a country's economic performance is its effective exchange rate. This should be distinguished from the 'nominal' exchange rate between one country's currency and another. Effective exchange rates are a weighted average of the home country's currency against those of the range of countries with which it trades. The weightings given to each foreign currency are based on their respective country's trade with the home country.

Hence if Britain had, for the sake of argument, 60% of its trade going to the Euro-zone, 25% to the US and 15% to Japan, the effective sterling rate would be calculated by weighting the movements in the Euro, the dollar and the yen accordingly. Effective rates are therefore expressed as index numbers rather than absolute values because they are a mixture of several different currencies.

Recent changes

Table 8.2 shows the movements in the actual and effective rates for various currencies in 2001.

Interpretation

What makes exchange rates move as they do? The answer is far from simple. Exchange rates move because of a number of factors.

These range from the underlying flows of trade; the legitimate hedging activities of companies to protect the value of their foreign currency revenue; through speculative movements based on market trends and vague geopolitical assumptions and theories; to interest rates relative to those of other financial centres; domestic inflation; and the perceived soundness of government debt in the currency concerned. Each factor pulls the currency in a slightly different direction. Some assume greater importance than others for a period and then fade from view.

Some currencies are more volatile than others. 'Reserve' currencies – those widely accepted for the international settlement of debts – may be harder to move than those of emerging markets. They are therefore less susceptible to (though not immune from) the depredations of speculators.

Speculation by hedge funds is believed to have played a part in the collapse of many Asian currencies in 1997/98. The catalyst for the collapses was weak economic performance, but the fact that speculation brought about the collapse of the currencies itself contributed to the problem. IMF intervention, it can be argued, made matters worse in many countries.

Lack of confidence in the currency, notwithstanding a semi-formal peg to the dollar, has also been responsible for political and economic turmoil in Argentina, the initial catalyst being the problem of servicing the country's huge foreign debt.

Table 8.2 Selected exchange rate data versus sterling

	Actual rate 2001				Effective rate 2001			
	Q1	Q2	Q3	Q4	Q1	Q2	Q3	Q4
Australian$	2.7525	2.7675	2.8013	2.8214	72.5	72.3	71.7	71.7
Canadian$	2.2284	2.1877	2.2199	2.2807	78.3	78.3	77.9	76.1
Danish Kr	11.7981	12.1436	12.0231	11.9888	102.1	101.4	102.2	102.5
Euro	1.5813	1.6280	1.6152	1.6112	79.8	77.6	78.4	78.8
HK$	11.3765	11.0866	11.2092	11.2546	0	0	0	0
Japanese yen	172.3700	174.0800	174.7100	178.1800	140.9	138.9	138.9	136.5
NZ$	3.3753	3.4275	3.4292	3.4743	80.4	79.5	79.9	79.4
Saudi riyal	5.4704	5.3267	5.3900	5.4119	0	0	0	0
S African rand	11.4104	11.4149	12.0471	14.6257	0	0	0	0
Sterling (vs US$)	0.6857	0.7042	0.6960	0.6931	104.5	106.4	106.1	106.1
Swedish Kr	14.2324	14.8531	15.1923	15.2648	78.2	76.2	74.2	73.7
Swiss Fr	2.4241	2.4881	2.4336	2.3743	108.0	107.3	109.3	112.0
US$	1.4586	1.4203	1.4371	1.4430	115.7	119.8	118.7	119.6

Source: Bank of England

Many solutions are prescribed for countries with chronically weak exchange rates. In Argentina, at the outset of the recent crisis, the putative solution included simply replacing the existing currency with US dollars, continuing with an independently managed currency board that would control the expansion of the monetary base more strictly than had been the case thus far, the creation of an entirely new currency, or devaluation. None of these options is painless. The latter was the eventual choice made.

Currency weakness usually (though not exclusively) in emerging markets is often the result of countries living beyond their means and borrowing too much. As is the case for any household, adjusting to good housekeeping after a binge can be protracted, painful and politically very difficult indeed.

S I D E B A R

What really moves currencies?

One theory often cited in the foreign exchange market suggests that currency movements are based around relative differentials in inflation rates. In other words, if US inflation is 3% and UK inflation is 1%, then the dollar should depreciate against sterling by 2% to make up the difference and equalize the true purchasing power between the two countries. This is known as the 'purchasing power parity' theory.

An analogous theory says that currency movements depend on relative interest rates. It claims that rational investors look for a total return on investment in any country that is based on the interest rates or risk-free bond yields on offer.

Higher bond yields or interest rates in one country compared with another will result in its currency attracting demand and rising in value up to the point where its expected future downward movement will equal the difference between the two rates of return.

Most observers reckon that the long-term value of currency reflects some mixture of these two theories, but that speculative flows in the market cause the value of the currency to swing, sometimes fairly violently, around what might objectively be considered its true worth.

There are periodic calls for speculative foreign exchange transactions to attract a small tax (known as the Tobin tax, after its original proponent, economist James Tobin), although since the tax would have to be universally applied to be effective, such calls are usually ignored.

Why is it important for you?

The most obvious impact of the external value of a country 's currency is felt when we go abroad.

If we live in a country with a hard currency, going abroad can be a pleasure. Our currency goes a long way and is readily accepted. At home, imported goods are cheap, although sometimes retailers may appropriate some of this cheapness into their profit and loss accounts rather than passing it on to us as consumers.

Living in a country with a weak currency is much less comfortable. The son of a friend of mine emigrated with his family to New Zealand partly because property seemed very cheap, only to find that wage rates were equally low and setting up a business was difficult because many of the products he wanted to sell had costs in dollars and pounds. The margins he expected to make were also eroded because an item that would have sold for £25 in the UK would remain unsold at half the price in New Zealand because disposable income was less.

Those with incomes and liquid assets in hard currency areas can take advantage of things like this, for example, by buying a holiday home or other physical assets, but it's rarely comfortable for everyone concerned.

Commodity prices

Definition

Like exchange rates, movements in the price of commodities are determined by the pull of supply and demand in the market.

Again like exchange rates, part of the demand for commodities reflects bona fide industrial use – food producers buying wheat and cocoa, car-makers buying platinum and copper, chemical companies buying oil, and so on. But there is also speculative demand, which from time to time can distort the price.

Alternative names

Like foreign exchange, commodities can be bought in a spot market, and also for delivery in physical form at various points in the future.

While futures markets are self-evidently tools for speculators, they are also a means by which producers of commodities can guarantee the prices they will receive for their output as and when it is produced.

Futures markets developed at the Chicago Board of Trade precisely because of the demand for farmers in the Midwest corn belt to be able to sell all or part of their crops forward to provide themselves with a guaranteed income and finance to buy seed and farm equipment. Later on, futures contracts on other farm-based products were added.

To some degree futures markets and spot markets in commodities have become so closely linked that it is hard to determine whether the spot price influences the futures price or the other way round. In other words, does the tail wag the dog?

In many commodities, as in many stock markets, it is the futures market that is by far the more liquid of the two. Different futures markets around the world specialize in – or more accurately have captured the liquidity in – different commodity futures contracts.

The important commodities that economists and other market watchers keep an eye on are:

■ precious metals – chiefly gold and platinum

■ base metals – particularly copper, nickel and aluminium

■ soft commodities – wheat, rice, coffee, cocoa

■ oil and gas.

Some market watchers also keep a close eye on shipping rates, which are also traded in spot and futures versions. Power is increasingly becoming a traded commodity, and one to watch for the future is trade in so-called 'emissions credits', in effect a market in pollution. There is now even trading in weather futures.

In particular countries or parts of countries, the prices of other commodities will assume greater importance, perhaps because they represent the staple crop produced in a particular area. Examples include rubber, tin, soybeans, cotton, pork, eggs and even orange juice.

How it's calculated

A market price is a market price, so there is little need to go into undue detail about how it is arrived at. What are worth noting, however, are those currencies in which commodities are expressed. In the main it tends to be the US dollar. Oil is traded in $ per barrel, gold in $ per fine ounce, and so on.

What this means is that the strength or weakness in the dollar relative to their own currency affects the revenue that producers earn from selling the commodities they produce.

Table 8.3 Selected statistics on commodity prices

All figures in US dollars per tonne, except oil, which is US dollars per barrel and gold which is in US dollars per ounce

End of:	2000				2001			
	Q1	Q2	Q3	Q4	Q1	Q2	Q3	Q4
Gold	276.10	288.10	273.60	272.60	257.70	270.00	293.10	277.70
Nickel	9940.00	8035.00	8265.00	6825.00	5785.00	5965.00	4832.00	5585.00
Copper	1764.00	1791.50	1995.50	1828.50	1687.00	1567.80	1445.00	1488.50
Aluminium	1551.50	1579.50	1594.80	1561.50	1491.50	1462.50	1337.50	1360.00
Oil	25.11	29.84	29.81	23.06	24.95	25.41	23.05	20.45

One reason for OPEC's unilateral action in raising the oil price in the early 1970s was as a direct response to weakness in the value of the dollar that followed the move to floating exchange rates in 1971. Producers saw the income they derived from sales drop off and acted accordingly.

For agricultural commodities and base metals, there has also been a move by market watchers to express their movement in terms of indices, weighting each commodity price change for the relative importance of that particular commodity in the economy. Publications like *The Economist* and investment banks like Goldman Sachs have devised indices that do precisely this, even though calculating them is fraught with difficulty.

One obvious problem is that devising an index has somehow to get round the problem of different densities of various commodities. A tonne of lead is different to a tonne of aluminium, and different again from a tonne of cocoa. Indices that try to weight for the importance of different commodities face the problem of literally comparing apples and oranges.

Recent changes

Tables 8.3 shows how the prices of certain key commodities changed during 2000 and 2001.

Interpretation

How you interpret changes in commodity prices depends to some degree on which commodity you take. Some have value as general indicators of economic or financial health, some because of their importance as raw materials for specific industrial sectors.

The cocoa price has little importance to the British economy as a whole, but it is important to chocolate producer Cadbury, for obvious reasons. The gold price, by contrast, has more significance as an overall indicator of confidence in the financial system. Oil fits somewhere between the two.

Let's summarize the important considerations to take into account when looking at the way prices of particular commodities move.

Gold: Although gold is used in some industrial processes – in jewellery and in the automotive and semiconductor industries – the price sometimes reflects more than the demand from these mundane uses.

Gold has traditionally been seen as a store of value. Because it is indestructible and universally known and accepted, it is favoured by those who feel that paper currencies are not to be trusted, particularly if inflation is likely to debase their value. Because of its high value relative to its weight, it is also an easily portable form of wealth.

The gold price reflects this 'bolt hole' role. At times of extreme financial and political uncertainty, the price of gold rises. There was an upturn in the price of gold at the time of the 11 September 2001 terrorist attacks in New York.

To some degree, however, the greater accessibility of financial markets has resulted in other instruments fulfilling this safe haven role: the US dollar in general, and US treasury bonds in particular. Gold's attractions are partly offset because it yields no income (unlike a Treasury bond) and has holding costs – it has be stored in a safe place and insured. This can be circumvented by use of the futures market, which avoids holding the physical metal.

Indeed, the advent of forward sales of gold and the introduction of gold futures and options have stabilized the price of gold. If the price rises sharply, forward sales of the metal typically kick in and depress the price.

Oil: The oil price has an important and measurable impact on the level of economic activity. A sustained increase in the oil price will reduce growth, increase inflation and worsen most countries' trade balance. A decrease in the oil price will do the reverse. When measuring this effect, the fact that oil is priced in dollars must be taken into account. It is the local currency oil price that is the important variable.

Sharp changes in the price of oil in the past have had effects that vary considerably from country to country. Japan is particularly reliant on imported energy and hence suffers more from an oil price rise. In the EU, consumer prices are likely to change more markedly if oil prices change than is the case in Japan or the US.

Crude oil is also an important feedstock for the chemical industry and has clear implications for the automotive industry. Government tax revenues depend in part on the oil price, as do the profits of companies selling products derived from oil, such as petrol and plastics.

> Movements in the copper price are generally regarded as a good indicator of turning points in the economy.

Copper: Movements in the copper price are generally regarded as a good indicator of turning points in the economy. While the price of gold and silver is influenced by thoughts of their use in the past as safe havens and their aesthetic value, there is no such baggage with copper.

Demand simply reflects its use as an industrial metal and hence an upturn in price will tend, other things being equal, to signify higher production and a reviving economy, not least perhaps because supplies will have to be bought in anticipation of higher production. To some degree, as with other metals, this neat relationship has been circumscribed by the advent of a futures market.

It also ignores the fact that for advanced economies, manufacturing is now a relatively small part of total economic activity. You might as well, a cynic would observe, look at the job advertisements for computer programmers or coffee bar 'baristas' for an indication of how the economy is doing.

Why is it important for you?

The importance of all these things for the man in the street tends to come down to their impact on the prices of everyday goods – petrol, perhaps, or our favourite chocolate bar, or the price of a cup of coffee – but enlightened and observant investors also watch them for signs that confirm, or contradict, what economists and economic statistics might be saying.

A suitably smoothed trend or an index of something that is determined by the actions of buyers and sellers in a marketplace is arguably a better indicator of what's happening than all the views of the pundits and the laboriously collected surveys and statistics produced by civil servants.

The drawback to using them is only that producers can also influence what happens to the price. Oil prices rise if producers agree on production cutbacks, and the same is true of metals. Here, a pick-up in the demand for copper may be masked by the fact that the price is still reflecting earlier overproduction by mines and high levels of stocks. The whole picture needs to be examined, although, since dealers do this, futures prices can take this into account.

Terms of trade

Definition

The terms of trade is shorthand for the ratio of export prices to import prices. They measure the purchasing power of a country's exports in terms of the imports they will buy.

Alternative names

The terms of trade is a long established concept. My 1960s vintage economics textbooks give the term substantial space, and it was around for many decades prior to that. There are few if any alternative ways of describing it.

How it's calculated

The conventional way of expressing the figure is the index of export prices divided by the index of import prices. This gives a figure that is more 'favourable' for the country concerned the higher the number. In some instances, notably in academic papers, the ratio is calculated in exactly the opposite way, in which case an improvement in the terms of trade is denoted by a fall rather than a rise in the ratio.

Recent changes

Terms of trade figures for the UK are given as part of the trade statistics published monthly around six to seven weeks after the end of the period in question. Table 8.4 gives data on terms of trade for the UK from 1999 to 2001.

Terms of trade are rarely given much importance in the US, partly because of the scale of the domestic economy relative to foreign trade, and partly because of the pivotal position of the dollar in international economics and the fact that many US raw material imports will be priced in dollars. It's perhaps also true that because Americans in general are relatively insular in their outlook, statistics like this are held to be of little account.

Interpretation

Interpreting the terms of trade accurately is no mean feat. Terms of trade figures are expressed in terms of price movements, but this is by no means the whole picture when it comes to trade.

For instance, commentators may speak of a deterioration in the terms of trade (imports getting more expensive relative to exports) but this may have a silver lining in terms of the trade balance, since small increases in export prices relative to those of competitors may lead to increased demand for exports. By the same token, if import prices go up, demand may fall.

Table 8.4 Statistics on UK terms of trade

Price indices (not seasonally adjusted)						
		Total			Total (ex oil)	
	Exports	Imports	Terms of trade	Exports	Imports	Terms of trade
1999 Q2	89.0	86.0	103.5	88.9	85.8	103.6
Q3	90.2	86.7	104.0	88.3	85.9	102.8
Q4	90.3	87.3	103.4	87.5	86.0	101.7
2000 Q1	90.7	88.2	102.8	87.0	86.4	100.7
Q2	91.9	89.1	103.1	87.7	87.2	100.6
Q3	94.2	91.2	103.3	88.6	88.5	100.1
Q4	94.9	92.0	103.2	88.8	89.2	99.6
2001 Q1	93.9	91.7	102.4	89.4	89.7	99.7
Q2	93.9	91.6	102.5	89.0	89.3	99.7
Q3	92.9	89.0	104.4	88.5	86.9	101.8
Q4	90.8	87.2	104.1	88.1	86.0	102.4

The overall effect of a worsening in the terms of trade could therefore be, paradoxically, an improvement in the balance of trade – an improvement in the value of exports relative to imports. And the reverse is of course true, in the case of a so-called 'improvement' in the terms of trade. It may lead to deterioration in the trade balance because exports are priced out of customers' reach, while imports appear cheaper to domestic consumers.

Another reason for being wary of placing too much emphasis on the terms of trade is that simply looking at this single number doesn't tell the whole story. An improvement in the terms of trade may be translated into bumper profits for exporters, but will it find its way back into the domestic economy?

Similarly, economists have long pondered the significance of currency changes on the terms of trade. A depreciating exchange rate will ostensibly worsen the terms of trade, but how much of an effect this has depends really on how responsive imports or exports are to changes in their price to domestic or foreign consumers respectively.

Why is it important for you?

The answer is that it probably isn't if you are a consumer and investor in a relatively affluent country. Changes in the terms of trade can have a much more marked effect on economies that are dependent on the price of a single product that is traded in markets outside their control. It is self-evident that this applies to many resource-based developing countries.

The problem for countries like this is that although the commodity they produce may be priced in dollars, their receipts may reflect the fact that they are selling to monopoly buyers in competition with other equally poor countries, while their imports, mainly from rich countries, will cost more if their exchange rate weakens. The course of the exchange rate may be tied up with perceptions about the commodity they produce, which in turn is traded outside their control.

Producers of coffee, cocoa and, to a lesser extent, some metals and minerals may well be in this position. Poor or worsening terms of trade is one of the main causes of poverty in the third world.

IN BRIEF

■ Due to the spread of globalization, foreign trade statistics are important to us all.

■ The balance of trade affects currencies and ultimately domestic interest rates.

■ There are many factors involved in exchange rate movements which assume various levels of importance at different times.

■ Currency exchange rates are also influenced by the actions of speculators and occasional government intervention.

■ Because of the rise in foreign travel we are all affected by exchange rates.

■ Commodity prices are expressed mainly in US dollars. A country's earnings are affected by its currency's strength or weakness against the dollar.

■ The prices of gold, oil and copper are particularly relevant for investors and economic forecasters.

■ Terms of trade are what a country's exports will buy in terms of imports.

■ Consumers in third world countries are generally affected more by adverse terms of trade than consumers in affluent countries.

chapter nine

Leading indicators and other stories

There are a number of other important indicators of economic health. Some of these attract the attention of the market and others do not. But all of them give a clue as to which way the economy is heading.

Retail sales are a primary indicator of consumer confidence. If consumers are confident enough to go out to the shops and spend money, arguably it speaks volumes more than any response they might give to a confidence survey.

Durable goods statistics come in a variety of guises. Orders for durable goods come from businesses (machinery, trucks) and from consumers (cars, washing machines). But statistics about orders and shipments are a good proxy for the confidence levels of businesses and consumers.

Housing market statistics have always had considerable significance in the UK, because of the average Brit's predilection for home ownership. In the US too, consumers have seen the rising value of their houses as collateral for borrowing to fund further consumption. Along with the stock market, it has been one of the props to the consumer society. Falling house prices hit consumer confidence and with it economic growth.

Advertising revenue is a key indicator of business confidence. Some businesses advertise through a recession, but many don't, at least until they sense that demand is starting to recover.

The stock market is often seen as a good discounter, or anticipator, of changes in economic activity or, more precisely, of corporate profitability. Its use as an indicator is muddied by extremes of emotion to which it is sometimes prone. But any student of the market needs to know how these indices work.

> Leading indicators are groups of indicators that over the years have predicted the course of the economy in advance.

Leading indicators are groups of indicators that over the years have predicted the course of the economy in advance. Some of the indicators described above fall into this category, whether or not they are included in the formal calculation of the index of leading indicators. But interpreting them needs some care.

Retail sales

Definition

Intuitively we all feel we know what constitutes retail sales, but there are nuances that need to be followed. Clearly retail sales are sales by retailers, normally presented in official statistics in the form of index numbers. For professional statistics watchers, most attention focuses on volume figures, that is, sales with the effect of price increases stripped out. Often, however, headline figures are figures for sales value, inflated by sales taxes such as VAT and excise duty.

Alternative names

Different countries have different names for the statistics gathered to show consumer behaviour at the retail level. The statistics vary depending on the comprehensiveness with which the retail waterfront is polled. In some European markets, for example, only sales through department stores are counted, while others exclude certain types of products, such as petrol, cars and alcohol.

In the popular mind, and often in the popular press, department store (or more broadly chain store) sales constitute retail sales, whereas they are in reality only a part of the picture.

How it's calculated

Retail sales statistics in most markets are calculated by means of survey data conducted each month. In the US, for example, some 13,000 businesses are asked to complete a report. It's generally the case in the majority of major markets that most of the crucial data will be provided by the large retail groups that represent the bulk of sales.

In the UK, the statistics are provided in index number format in a variety of ways, including the volume of sales (that's to say sales with the effect of inflation stripped out) and the value of sales, in both cases on a seasonally adjusted and unadjusted basis. The sales figures for the month are based on weekly averages. Quarterly numbers are weighted for differing numbers of weeks in each month.

Figures are divided into broad categories, for which indices are calculated separately. These include food stores, all non-food, textiles, clothing and footwear, household goods, other retailing, non-store retailing (i.e. mail order) and so on.

It goes without saying that most professional users of statistics use the seasonally adjusted figures for the value of retail sales as the key variable they analyze, although press comment sometimes focuses on absolute amounts and unadjusted figures.

Recent changes

Figures for retail sales are issued pretty promptly. In the UK, the retail sales release appears in the middle of the month following the one for which figures are being published (i.e. a couple of weeks after the period end). For example, figures for November retail sales will be issued in mid-December.

Table 9.1 shows trends in retail sales in the UK in 2001 and early 2002.

Interpretation

Retail sales are clearly an important component of demand in the economy at large, but they aren't the be-all and end-all. In round figures and other things being equal, a gain of 1% in retail sales will translate into a 0.3% increase in GDP. Consumers are fickle, however, and there are several factors that can distort retail sales.

Any sort of external shock, such as terrorist attack, political change, financial collapse, death of a leading politician or royalty, might make consumers disengage from any form of shopping for a short while, or at least a sufficient number of them for a blip to show up in the figures. On the other hand, there is a school of thought that disaster can produce spending binges, again on a temporary basis.

While figures may be seasonally adjusted, they cannot take account of abnormally warm or cold weather, either of which may have an adverse impact on sales. Price promotional activity by large retailers can also influence sales.

Table 9.1 Statistics on seasonally adjusted UK retail sales

| | | Volume 1995 = 100 | Year-on-year percentage change | |
			Volume	Value*
2001	September	129.4	6.1	7.3
	October	129.5	6.0	6.2
	November	131.1	7.1	6.8
	December	130.6	5.7	6.8
2002	January	130.6	4.7	5.5
	February	132.0	5.8	6.3
	March	132.1	5.6	6.7

*not seasonally adjusted

Source: National Statistics

The other important point is that service sector sales are not included in retail sales figures if the services are not purchased at a retail outlet. While buying a book from Amazon might show up in retail sales via the mail order category, buying a computer direct from Dell probably wouldn't. What you pay your accountant or solicitor doesn't show up in retail sales either.

Why is it important for you?

From the standpoint of investors, retail sales can be a good guide to the performance of individual sectors, albeit somewhat after the event. Sales figures are clearly a good guide to the performance of retailers, but also to the sectors that supply them. Shifts in spending between sectors are also something of a guide to the state of the economy.

When times are tough consumers spend more on necessities and basic luxuries and less on luxuries and big-ticket items such as cars. Watching these different trends can give you some idea of the robustness or otherwise of the economy as a whole.

A pick-up in sales of durable goods demand is often seen as a particularly good leading indicator for the economy and therefore a trigger for stock market analysts to begin viewing life with even greater optimism.

Car production and sales

Definition

The distinction between production and sales of cars is fairly obvious. The sales figures used are normally those relating to new cars expressed in numbers of units. In the case of production statistics, official figures are also given in terms of numbers of vehicles produced, with these also expressed as index numbers.

Car sales and production levels are a sensitive indicator of economic performance. Apart from housing, buying a car is probably one of the biggest purchasing decisions a consumer will make.

In any major world economy, sales of new cars are therefore a good indicator of prosperity and confidence, both for businesses and consumers.

Vehicle production statistics can be slightly distorted by the fact that cars produced in a country may be exported, while those bought may include imported models. Equally, dealers' and manufacturers stock levels can influence the level of production.

Alternative names

In the US, statistics related to cars are normally referred to as 'auto' sales. Statistics of 'auto' production, as distinct from sales, are normally available (as in the UK) as monthly data and are a subset of industrial production numbers.

The term 'assembly rate' is also often used in US auto production data. This is the annualized monthly production rate, seasonally adjusted. Assembly rates are usually compared with sales and stock levels to see whether current levels of production are sustainable.

How it's calculated

In both the UK and the US, production figures for vehicles are produced by official statistical organizations as part of the process of compiling industrial production statistics. The method used is primarily through surveys of manufacturers. In the case of car production this is relatively easy, since there are so few domestic manufacturers. Production figures normally show home and export sales in both index number form and in absolute terms.

Car (or 'auto') sales figures are published in both cases by trade bodies representing motor vehicle producers and dealers. In Britain this is the Society of Motor Manufacturers and Traders (or SMMT) and in the US the American Automobile Manufacturers' Association. Data from the SMMT can be found at **www.smmt.co.uk**.

Recent changes

Statistics for motor vehicle production are issued by National Statistics on a monthly basis about 21 days after the end of the month in question. Data from the SMMT on new car registrations is generally produced five or six days after the end of the month in question and shows a variety of statistics, including sales broken down by type of customer, by manufacturers, the top ten models, import penetration and a variety of other data.

Statistics for the UK market in 2001 and early 2002 are shown in Tables 9.2 and 9.3.

Interpretation

In late 2001 there was a sharp upward movement in new car sales in the US, a statistic that got investors and commentators particularly excited. On more mature reflection the figures proved to be less meaningful than they might have been, because they reflected aggressive discounting by dealers to shift inventory, and also came at a time when credit was readily available and interest rates low.

This neatly illustrates the dilemma in interpreting vehicle production and sales figures. They are sensitive economic indicators, but they are influenced by a number of variables in the economy, any one of which can have a big influence on any particular month's figures.

Probably one of the best ways of looking at figures like this is to take two or three months' figures together and to compare them with the same period of the previous year, or else to use a moving average as a way of establishing the trend.

In the UK, the timing of new registration plates has long been seen as an influence over car sales, originally bunching sales into August and now into March and September. This needs to be taken into account when trying to read the figures.

Table 9.2 Statistics on seasonally adjusted UK motor vehicle production

1995 = 100	Total production	Home	Export	Commercial vehicles
2001 June	100	69	126	84
July	96	61	123	87
August	108	97	135	118
September	101	80	126	95
October	102	81	122	86
November	100	71	123	77
December	105	87	123	81
% change in last months on:				
previous three months	−5.3	4.8	6.5	−1.7
same period last year	12.3	12.8	11.3	−6.6

Source: SMMT

Table 9.3 Statistics on UK new car registrations

New registrations	March 2002 All cars	% change
Month	423727	3.9
Year to date	722718	7.1
Last three months	722718	7.1

Source: SMMT

It's also worth noting that there is a business investment aspect to vehicle production. Sales of cars to private individuals are counted as part of consumption. Fleet car sales can be treated as business investment, as can sales of trucks. In the US, however, the popularity of so-called sports utility vehicles (SUVs), which are categorized at present as light trucks, has to be taken into account when looking at the figures.

There is another aspect to this. While new car sales are an important indicator of demand, and vehicle production figures are fairly unambiguous, the structure of the industry complicates matters when it comes to determining the overall impact of the UK car industry on the economy as a whole. This is because there may be imported components in cars produced by UK manufacturers and vice versa. Components made in the UK may be shipped to the same company's factories elsewhere in Europe, and similarly components imported from abroad may be assembled into finished vehicles in Britain. Where this process begins and ends may be hard to discern from the figures.

> It's also worth noting that there is a business investment aspect to vehicle production.

Why is it important for you?

Is it important for you? It may not be. New car registrations are one of a range of economic indicators that are not so much interesting in their own right but used as a signal to predict turning points in the economy and hence in the stock market. These are called leading indicators. We'll look at the importance of different leading indicators later in this chapter.

Housing market statistics

Definition

The housing statistics traditionally used as an indicator of economic activity are housing starts, that's to say, the numbers of new houses on which construction has begun in any particular month. Housing completions figures are also provided on a monthly basis. Similar statistics are closely watched in other markets, particularly the US.

As most people in the UK already own their own homes, there is also considerable interest in trends in house prices. Rival building societies in the UK – Nationwide and Halifax – compete to release surveys of house price activity each month based on data from their respective branches.

Alternative names

Names of housing statistics are refreshingly straightforward. Some US statistics cover new housing permits, the equivalent of planning permissions in the UK.

How it's calculated

A start is counted from the day the ground is broken to begin the foundations, not before. The figures for new housing starts and completions are collected from building control statistics provided by local councils. In the US this system is broadly similar except for areas where there is no building control regime, when on-site surveys are used instead.

House price statistics are derived from building society branches and generally reflect the prices at which sales are completed, rather than asking prices. Because of their extensive branch networks, building societies are well placed to estimate trends in prices and other aspects of the housing market, such as the volume of activity and trends in different price brackets and regions.

Table 9.4 Statistics for seasonally adjusted UK housing starts and completions (in thousands)

		Total starts	Total completions
2001	January	16.4	14.7
	February	14.1	13.2
	March	13.8	13.8
	April	13.8	13.3
	May	15.8	13.7
	June	15.1	12.8
	July	15.0	13.6
	August	14.9	13.3
	September	14.4	12.2
	October	16.5	15.0
	November	15.6	14.9
	December	12.9	9.7
% change latest quarter:			
versus previous quarter		3	6
versus same quarter last year		11	2

Source: DETR

Recent changes

Table 9.4 shows data for the UK in 2001 for housing starts and for completions. Both are issued on a monthly basis. House price data from building societies is generally available a week or so after the end of the relevant month.

Housing starts data is collected by the Department for Transport, local government and the regions, and is published about five weeks after the end of the month in question. As an example, data for October would be published in the first week in December, data for November in the first week in January, and so on.

Interpretation

Housing starts are a good indicator of levels of activity in the economy even though their impact on GDP is minimal. Sales of existing houses have no impact on economic growth since they simply reflect transfer of ownership from one person to another.

The problem with housing starts is that the data is acknowledged to be volatile. Construction activity is highly sensitive to weather and even the normal seasonal adjustment techniques cannot eliminate this aspect completely from the figures. Similarly, although figures are provided that break down housing starts by type of developer, it is often hard for the statistics to pick up whether or not particular projects are being built for private or social housing, since a developer may work on both types of housing project.

It's also worth bearing in mind, before reading too much into the figures, that housing starts reflect other factors in addition to the general level of economic activity, chiefly interest rates and therefore the availability and price of finance for new buyers, and also simple population growth and population structure. House prices themselves are linked to activity in the housing market. Increasing prices may increase the willingness of people to move house or buy a new house rather than rent. Falling prices tend to dampen activity.

Why is it important for you?

An Englishman's home is his castle, as the saying goes. It has long been known that the British in particular have a predilection for geared-up investment in the property market through home ownership purchased on a mortgage. It happens in the UK to a much greater degree than is the case in some other countries. Trends in house prices in particular are therefore a crucial barometer. Movements in house prices produce a 'wealth effect' on consumption.

This has reached much more outlandish stages in the US, because of the ease of mortgage refinancing. As interest rates have fallen and house prices have risen, Americans have flocked to refinance their mortgages, cash in some equity and go shopping, a factor which has helped support the economy during the period of declining stock prices.

You can take your own view about whether or not this is wise or healthy. Mortgages in the US are typically at rates that are fixed by reference to the yield on ten-year government bonds. This gives American consumers another opportunity to feed their obsession with the stock market by watching bond prices as well as the prices of their stocks.

Advertising

Definition

Advertising is a good informal indicator of the state of business confidence.

Statistics are not published in a form that is readily available to investors, but advertising trade associations, such as the Advertising Association in the UK (**www.adassoc.org.uk**), publish figures regularly, typically of advertising spending. The Advertising Association's yearbook has detailed figures.

In the US, various statistics are produced, but the ones that are most closely watched are those that show where companies have cancelled options to take out ads in the future.

Alternative names

Although this is not applicable, as a freelance journalist I have found that my income from placing articles with newspapers and magazines has tracked trends in advertising fairly closely.

Many newspapers and magazines function with a fixed level of permanent staff and use freelance writers to supplement this team where necessary. Rising advertising revenue produces bigger issues and hence more demand for editorial copy, and more work for me and those like me. Conversely, at times when advertising is shrinking, freelance contributors are the first to feel it.

How it's calculated

Advertising revenue is measured in terms of monetary value and the statistics are fairly crude. There are no attempts at seasonal adjustments. Figures for cancelled options may also be given in the same way.

Recent changes

Table 9.5 gives some advertising statistics for 2000 in the UK.

Interpretation and why it's important for you

Lord Leverhulme, when asked about advertising, remarked that he knew that half the money his company (Lever Brothers) spent on advertising was wasted, but the problem was that he didn't know which half.

Companies will almost always take the view that some advertising is necessary. But they may shift the ways in which they spend it or spend more on promotional activities that have been demonstrated to produce more tangible results in the form of firm orders.

2000 was a banner year for advertising in the US, but 2001 saw a steep decline as the economy went into reverse. The steepest decline in spending was seen in national TV advertising spots and in broadcast syndication. By contrast, newspapers and to a lesser degree magazines saw declines in spending that were much less steep.

At the time of writing, the decline in magazine advertising spending was expected to be steeper in 2002, but the drop in almost all other categories was expected to moderate from the declines seen in 2001. Some of the reduction in TV advertising spending may have fed back into cinema.

Table 9.5 UK advertising industry statistics

Analysis of spending on advertising in 2000 by media (£m)		
	Display	*Classified*
TV	4646	0
National press	1711	546
Regional press	919	1844
Consumer magazines	591	158
Business press	758	512
Directories	868	
Outdoor and transport	823	0
Radio	595	0
Cinema	128	0
Direct mail	2049	0
Internet	155	0

Source: Advertising Association

Predictions like this are fairly easy to make because advertisers have to make decisions about advertising space on TV some way ahead, typically about ten weeks before the start of a particular quarter. At the time of writing, cancellations were running at substantially lower levels than at the same point of the previous year.

One potentially misleading factor is that advertising relating to shifting unwanted merchandise or excess stock may account for a mid-recession upturn in advertising.

One good indicator of advertising health is easy for the average investor to spot. Go into any high street newsagent and feel the weight of high-profile business magazines or the size of job supplements in national newspapers. If the issues are thin, advertising is slack.

For the record, at the time I was writing the first draft of this book (December 2001) my freelance commissions from national newspapers and business magazines, having seen a flurry in October/November, had turned slack again, perhaps suggesting that the recession could have another downward leg. There is one welcome contrast with the last recession. Though some payments have slowed, I have experienced no bad debts (yet) from publications that went bust still owing me money. But that's probably a reflection of my rather tighter credit control procedures.

Stock market indices

Definition

Stock market indices measure the changes in a selected group of share prices and are used as benchmarks against which to measure the performance of individual shares, investment funds and even the economy as a whole.

All major stock markets have their own benchmark index, as well as (usually) a range of sub-indices. Often major stock markets will have a narrow index based on 100 shares or less, and a broad index based on 500 shares or more.

Alternative names

In the UK, the narrow and broad indices are respectively the FTSE 100 and FTSE All Share Indices. In the US, the respective indices would be the Dow Jones Industrial Average (an index of 30 leading blue chips) and the S&P 500. In France, the stock market index is called the CAC 40 and in Germany, the DAX, a 30-share benchmark.

The past few years has seen a proliferation of indices designed to measure specific market sectors or international groupings. There are several indices that cover pan-European blue chips and some that cover large companies globally. There are some that try to isolate specific investment themes, such as ethical investing.

Table 9.6 gives some basic data on leading stock market indices.

How it's calculated

Investors need to pay attention to the way stock market indices are calculated. In the main, indices are arithmetic averages of the market capitalizations of their constituents. In other words, each minute-by-minute value is found by multiplying each of the constituents' shares in issue by its share price, adding all the resulting values together and dividing by the number of constituents.

This means that the bigger the company in terms of its market value, the more influence a change in its share price will have on the change in the index value.

Sometimes index creators try to interfere with these rules to stop big companies dominating the index. Methods used include introducing a cap on the weighting that any one company can have, or only counting for the purpose of their weighting in the index the proportion of the shares that are not 'tightly held' by family or other major corporate shareholders.

> Sometimes index creators try to interfere with these rules to stop big companies dominating the index.

Index compilers have moved away from creating indices on the basis of geometric averages because of the disproportionate impact a collapse in the value of one constituent can have on the index as a whole. In a geometric index, which is calculated as the 'n'th root of the product of all the 'n' constituents of an index, if the value of

Table 9.6 Some basic data on leading stock market indices

Index name	Number of constituents	Country
FTSE 100	100	UK
FT30	30	UK
DJStoxx 50	50	World
DJ EuroStoxx	30	Europe
DAX	30	Germany
CAC40	40	France
Dow Jones	30	USA
Nikkei225	225	Japan

one constituent is zero, mathematical convention dictates that the product is zero and hence the index itself is zero. This is clearly unsatisfactory.

How the constituents themselves change over time to allow for the waxing or waning of the corporations themselves and for mergers and bankruptcies is an important part of interpreting an index. The sidebar explains how it works in the case of the FTSE 100 index.

S I D E B A R

Index heroes and villains

Four times a year, the chairmen and chief executives of big companies wait anxiously to find out whether their company has secured a coveted place in the FTSE 100 index. The places are coveted because membership of the index means that index tracker funds will buy the company's shares, often boosting the price. There's also the small matter that executive pay is appreciably better at FTSE 100 companies.

But the way in which these changes are made can sometimes seem opaque. So how and why do they happen?

The FTSE 100 was started largely for the benefit of futures traders, to give them an index benchmark that was easy to calculate and representative of the UK equity market as a whole. So although they might appear opaque, the rules governing changes in the index have to be transparent and predictable, even if they are complicated.

An independent committee administers them. It has representatives from the *Financial Times*, the London Stock Exchange, market users, LIFFE (the London International Financial Futures and Options Exchange) and the Institute of Actuaries. The committee meets quarterly, or more frequently if necessary. Its procedures cover rules for inclusion and exclusion of particular companies, and what happens in the event of takeovers, right issues, new issues and suspensions.

In the case for the procedure for inclusion in the list, the ideal is for the index to contain the largest 100 companies by market capitalization at any one time. However, because this is capable of changing on a daily basis, the list is reviewed quarterly and a 90/110 rule adopted. This means that any company whose market capitalization has risen to the 90th position or above is automatically included. Any that has fallen below 110th place is excluded. Constituents that are then between 101 and 110 may be removed to make room for the stock or stocks that have a higher capitalization. In addition there is a reserve list of stocks to take account of changes that may need to be made between reviews because of takeovers or suspensions.

Changes to the list are publicized in advance and normally operate from the first business day following the expiry of the FTSE 100 index futures and options contracts (this happens on the third Friday of March, June, September and December).

In the case of mergers and takeovers, the vacant place is filled from the reserve list. This applies even if the takeover has been of one index constituent by another.

It is only rarely that a newly floated company will be large enough to qualify for inclusion in the index. In these instances, however (mmO^2 was the most recent example, displacing United Business Media), the new stock will qualify for automatic membership of the index.

Membership of the index requires a substantial market capitalization. The current threshold for a company to qualify for automatic inclusion in the index was a total market value for its shares in the region of £2.3bn.

Recent changes

Figures 9.1 and 9.2 show recent changes in the value of the FTSE 100 Index and the S&P 500.

Figure 9.1 Graph of FTSE 100 Index

Source: Sharescope

Interpretation

Stock market indices are important because the stock market is supposedly a perfect discounting mechanism. This is another way of saying that it tends to anticipate changes in the health of the corporate sector as a whole.

However, the connection is far from perfect and has been found particularly wanting in the case of technology companies in all markets across the world. Technology shares as a whole are not worth 50% or 75% less than they were in March 2001; it is simply that perceptions of their true underlying value have come back more in line with reality. There are those who say that those perceptions are still unduly rose-tinted and that a further downward reassessment may be in order.

It has only served to flag the point that stock markets are illogical and that placing too much reliance on them may be unwise.

Interpreting the way in which market indices behave on any given day or week is also fraught with danger. One reason that market indices like the FTSE 100 were created was because they could be used as the basis for futures and options that derived from their value. The value of trading in these derivatives far outstrips the value of the underlying market, and in many cases it is derivatives trading that has driven the value of the index, and not the other way round.

Figure 9.2 Graph of S&P 500 Index

Source: Sharescope

Similarly, the growth of index tracker funds has also contributed to this volatility. Such funds have to buy the constituents of an index to ensure their performance mimics the way the index moves. If new companies enter the index, the funds have to buy them, which drives up their price, and the index itself, in what is essentially a self-fulfilling process.

Interpreting stock markets is a complex process, but stock market analysts often use devices such as moving averages, trend lines and regression analysis to find patterns in the market and to spot turning points. This is a huge subject in its own right, beyond the scope of this book.

Why is it important for you?

Like car sales, the yield curve, housing starts and other statistics, how stock market indices behave is rightly or wrongly normally considered as a leading indicator of the economy. There are those who say that it is the best and indeed only real-time indicator of consumer confidence there is.

More important perhaps, what happens to the markets affects any of us who have pension funds or investments in unit trusts and other collective investment vehicles.

In the US, the stock market has come to be a particularly crucial economic variable. Americans as a group have a lot of their savings tied up in the stock market, and the course of the stock market can dictate the level of savings and borrowing and the degree to which consumers are confident about their jobs and the future.

There is an argument for saying that this obsession has gone too far and that it ultimately will exert a drag on the real economy for many years. There is no doubt that it presents the authorities with a problem. They want to wean the consumer away from undue dependence on the stock market and back into greater prudence, but if they go out of their way to burst the bubble, the remedy may prove to be worse than the disease, with wholesale bankruptcies and a slump in economic activity.

Composite leading indicators

Definition

Many of the statistics quoted elsewhere in this chapter, and some elsewhere in this book, are leading indicators of economic activity. Composite leading indicators take a group of leading indicators and measure their combined signals. They are used to try to predict the course of the economic cycle.

The rationale is that certain statistics tend to lead changes in economic activity. So by watching these and adding together their signals, we can get some idea of how the economy might perform in the near future.

Alternative names

Leading indicators are a well-known phenomenon and statistics on leading indicators are published in many markets, including the UK and the US. Leading indicators should not be confused with figures for coincident indicators (for example GDP), or lagging indicators (employment and unemployment, for example).

How it's calculated

The US system for compiling leading indicators, masterminded by the independent private sector research organization the Conference Board, is a good one to study because it has been consistently good at predicting changes in activity. The Conference Board also produces figures for leading, coincident and lagging indicators for the UK, Germany and other major economies. More detail on the data is at **www.globalindicators.org**.

The indicators used in the US and elsewhere are chosen on the basis of several different criteria. These are primarily related to their consistency and reliability as indicators, the accuracy and timeliness of the data, the relatively limited nature of any subsequent revisions to the data, and the fact that they move in relatively smooth ways. These attributes are also sought in measures of lagging and coincident indicators.

S I D E B A R

US leading indicators and why they are chosen

In compiling the US index, which looks at month-by-month changes rather than absolute amounts, each of the ten indicators in the index is assigned a weighting based on its importance. The weighting is also adjusted for the month-by-month volatility of the measurement in question. This means that a more volatile indicator, whose volatility might contribute to a false reading of the composite indicator, is given a lower weighting than it might otherwise have had.

The precise calculation is complex and not strictly relevant to the interpretation of the index. But the statistics used as leading indicators are revealing. They are:

- average weekly hours in manufacturing
- average weekly initial jobless claims
- manufacturers' new orders for consumer goods and materials at constant prices
- speed of suppliers' deliveries to manufacturers
- new orders for non-defence-related capital goods
- new housing permits
- S&P 500 index
- M2 money supply at constant prices
- the yield spread between money market rates and ten-year government bonds
- index of consumer expectations.

All of these make sense as variables that might proceed ahead of a change in economic activity. Many of them have been covered in earlier chapters. If recession is imminent, hours worked will be cut and companies may start to lay people off, prompting new unemployment claims, consumer confidence will fall, fewer new houses will be built.

Speed of deliveries from suppliers to manufacturers will increase in an incipient recession, since they will have fewer orders and will be able to produce for existing customers more quickly.

The fact that money supply, the stock market and the yield spread are included, however, might be regarded as debasing the currency somewhat. The yield spread and money supply can be influenced by government action (cutting rates, making credit easier), while the stock market is famously given to extremes of illogic.

Calculations of leading indicators are not the same from country to country. In the UK, for example, the index of leading indicators comprises eight sets of data. These are: money supply, share prices, changes in inventories, the bond yield spread, housing starts, the volume of export orders, consumer confidence and new orders in engineering.

For comparison, UK coincident indicators are personal disposable income, industrial production, retail sales and the unemployment rate. In the US, the statistics used as coincident indicators are non-farm employment, industrial production, personal disposable income (PDI) and manufacturing and trade sales.

Recent changes

The Conference Board releases data on composite economic indicators like this according to a regular monthly schedule, with the figures normally produced around the middle of the month following the one to which they apply.

By way of example, table 9.7 shows Conference Board data for both the UK and US for November 2001.

Interpretation and why it's important for you

There is a big temptation to ascribe to a leading indicator an importance that it does not warrant. This is particularly so since, despite attempts by index compilers to give less importance to volatile data, a sharp reduction in short-term interest rates or a sharp increase in share prices can outweigh some of the more mundane statistical data that might actually be a better guide to events in the real economy.

The way to get round this is to wait until there have been two or three consecutive months' change in the data in the same direction. While prudence might dictate this, few stock market strategists wait that long. Most are ready to call the turn in the economy on the strength of one or two months' data, even if they have to backtrack at a later date.

It's also worth remembering that the components of the index may not turn simultaneously. Interest rates normally trough about 18 months after a peak in GDP, while business confidence, share prices and housing starts might peak anywhere from eight months to a year ahead of a peak in activity, at least in a normal cycle. Retail sales are said to lead economic activity by a month or two.

And not all cycles are the same. The most recent downturn in activity has been investment and inventory led rather than consumer led, and business confidence collapsed late and exceptionally quickly. Moreover, the downturn was based in one sector (technology) and spread from there to many others.

Table 9.7 Conference Board data on UK and US leading indicators

UK data for November 2001		US data for November 2001	
Current value	114.5	Current value	109.7
Percent change this month	0.2	Percent change this month	0.5
Percent change last month	−0.5	Percent change last month	0.1
Percent change prior month	−0.8	Percent change prior month	−0.5
Percent below recent peak	−4.2 Feb 01	Percent below recent peak	n/a

Source: Conference Board

It is the changes in direction in leading indicators that are important, but the precision involved is such that it's likely to be a good idea to seek confirmation from other sources before going overboard that recovery is underway or, at the end of a period of economic growth, that a downturn has started.

Remember, too, that an upturn in a composite of leading indicators does not imply anything about the strength or otherwise or the duration of the upturn that it portends.

IN BRIEF

- Retail sales and trends in them can provide a good guide to the state of the economy.

- New car sales and production are influential statistics but subject to numerous outside influences due to the international nature of the industry.

- House price statistics are particularly important indicators in the UK due to a long-standing predilection for home ownership.

- Stock market indices reflect the economic state of the corporate sector but are often illogical. They are, however, a good real-time indicator of consumer confidence.

- Calculations of leading indicators vary from country to country. The US system has been particularly good at predicting the state of the economy.

Oddball indicators

Not all of the indicators that investors use to determine the level of the market or the true value of a company are based on sober statistical analysis. This chapter looks at a selection of some of the more offbeat ones (there are many more that could be used). Many are of US origin and work best (though not exclusively) with US data.

Most are rooted in the shrewd observation of investor behaviour over the course of many market cycles. Others take everyday items and convert them into indicators that work. They work often because they describe well a set of underlying economic relationships. Table 10.1 gives a quick summary.

The 'Big Mac' index devised by *The Economist* compares the dollar value of hamburgers in different countries and attempts to show whether or not the currency of the country in question is over or undervalued against the dollar. The basis for this is the natural assumption that if McDonald's had its way, a hamburger would cost the same in purchasing power terms whatever market it were to be sold in.

Table 10.1 Some of the more off beat indicators

Theory	Measures
Big Mac	Over or undervaluation of currencies on purchasing power parity (PPP) basis
Hemline	Over or undervaluation of stock market
Cocktail Party	Over or undervaluation of stock market
R-word	Current position in economic cycle
Odd-lot	Over or undervaluation of the stock market
Put–call ratio	Over or undervaluation of the stock market
Stock market/GDP	Over or undervaluation of the stock market
Tobin's Q	Over or undervaluation of the stock market

The Hemline index relates the level of the stock market to the shortness or otherwise of women's skirts. If the fashion is for shorter skirts, the market is set for a rise; if hemlines plunge, the chances are the market will do so too.

Fund manager Peter Lynch, in his book *One Up on Wall Street*, (Simon & Shuster, 2000) also describes the Cocktail Party theory. That people pestered him for tips at cocktail parties was a sure sign of a bull market. Only when he was snubbed at parties was a bear market at its nadir.

Another indicator, used by several newspapers, counts the number of times the word 'recession', the so-called R-word, is mentioned in newspaper articles over a particular period. Normally mention of the recession reaches a peak just as the recession is ending.

Many other market indicators exploit the fact that historically the behaviour of private investors has been a classic 'contrary signal' to professionals. The market has no shortage of cynics. One of the more cynical observations of professional investors is that the private investor is generally wrong about the market. In other words, whatever the private investor is doing, particularly if it is being done with great enthusiasm, it is usually right to do the opposite.

The market has no shortage of cynics.

In broad terms this is called the contrary opinion theory. But it has spawned a wide range of specific theories and indicators used to measure the way investors are behaving. Many use data that can be combined in particular ways to quantify the essence of that all-important 'market sentiment' factor.

The odd-lot theory suggests that activity in odd lots of shares (i.e. orders of less than 100 shares in US terminology) measures the trading of small private investors, who are unable to afford bigger parcels of stock. When odd-lot activity is at a high level, the chances are that the smallest of investors are buying (or selling) with misplaced enthusiasm and the smart money should do the opposite.

Another variant of this is the put–call ratio. This measures the volume of put options traded relative to the number of call options. Put options, options to sell shares or a stock market index value at a fixed price or level for a specified period of time are normally employed when investors expect the market to fall. Call options are the reverse, used when an investor expects the market to rise. If the volume of puts traded exceeds the volume of calls, then the market might reasonably be expected to fall. However, the contrary opinion theory comes into play here too. Extreme spikes in the put–call ratio usually indicate that it might be a good idea to do the opposite to the crowd.

Some broader market indicators relate the level of the stock market to the real economy. One common way of doing this is to compare the capitalization of the stock market (i.e. the market value of all companies listed) to the size of the economy as measured by GDP. There are some drawbacks to using this ratio, which we'll come to later, but it is extremely valuable for getting some historical perspective.

Similar comments apply to the so-called Tobin's Q ratio. This essentially compares the level of the stock market with the value of the net assets of the companies listed on it. Again there are problems with interpreting this ratio because of changes over time in the way companies themselves function, but it can add some valuable perspective.

Unlike some of the statistical measures that we've looked at earlier in the book, none of these indicators is wholly (or in some cases at all) based on data that is released by statistical organizations. It's more a case of looking for press comment about them or finding out the data for yourself from the stock market statistics published in daily financial newspapers such as the *Financial Times* and *The Wall Street Journal*.

With that in mind, let's have a look at how they work.

The Big Mac index

Definition

The Big Mac indicator, devised by *The Economist* magazine, is a way of illustrating how purchasing power parity works.

In a previous chapter we looked at what exchange rates can tell us. There is an argument for saying that the true value of an exchange rate is not necessarily the value it has on the foreign exchange market but what the average resident of that country can buy with the currency concerned. This is called the purchasing power parity value of the currency. It is a concept that has long been recognized by economists as another way of determining the 'true' value of a currency.

In the case of *The Economist's* Big Mac index the assumption is made that the price of a Big Mac would ordinarily be equally affordable in whatever country it is sold. The price in local currency compared with the dollar price, when translated at the normal exchange rate to the dollar, should indicate whether or not the currency's market value is above or below its purchasing power parity.

Alternative names

There is no alternative, although purchasing power parity is the name of the underlying concept.

How it's calculated

The local price of a Big Mac is divided by the dollar price to produce a 'Big Mac' based purchasing power parity rate of exchange. This is then compared with the actual rate.

Assume the sterling price of a Big Mac is £1.49 and the dollar price is $1.99. Not being a Big Mac fan I have no way of knowing whether these figures are correct or not! On this assumption, though, this produces a PPP rate of exchange of 0.748, equivalent to a rate of exchange expressed in the conventional way (i.e. $ per £) of £1 = $1.336. The actual rate of exchange in the market is £1 = $1.45, suggesting that the pound is overvalued and should actually buy fewer dollars per pound, at least based on the price of hamburgers.

Recent changes

At the time of writing, some of the most recent changes in the index, as published in *The Economist* in an issue in April 2002, showed Britain's currency as overvalued on a PPP basis, at least as defined by the price of a hamburger, by around 16%. Switzerland and Denmark also showed up as overvalued. Russia, Argentina and South Africa appeared the most undervalued. The Euro showed up as slightly undervalued.

Approximately two years prior to this (in January 2000) the same calculation showed Israel, Britain and Japan similarly overvalued, sterling by around 25%, the Euro area slightly overvalued, and Malaysia, Hungary and China the cheapest places to go.

Interpretation and why it's important for you

There are problems with the Big Mac index, but it provides an easy-to-understand indicator of the relative value of currencies. PPP purists would, of course, use a broader basket of goods to measure PPP accurately.

The other point to make of course is that distortions in the price of beef in different local markets because of tariff barriers and other factors, not to mention the differing effects of local sales taxes (such as VAT in the UK), labour costs and restaurant rental costs, will also affect the price of a humble burger.

According to *The Economist*, however, the Big Mac index came into its own at the time the Euro was launched, indicating an overvaluation that the market as a whole chose to ignore at its peril. PPP is a concept that works over the long term rather than the short term, but it does not pay to ignore the signals it sends.

The Hemline index

Definition

In the most common usage this indicator suggests that short skirts equate to a high market and plunging hemlines suggest a bear market ahead.

Alternative names

None.

How it's calculated

Want to gauge where hemlines are? Just go to your local high street and examine the evidence.

Recent changes

Consultation with my wife and business partner suggests that hemlines currently indicate the middle stages of a bear market. If next year's winter fashion collections suggest that long skirts are making a comeback, the theory would suggest that there is more pain ahead for the stock market.

Interpretation

Interpretation of the Hemline index can be tricky. There are a couple of caveats. An alternative version of the theory suggests that skirts get shorter and men's ties get narrower in a recession because manufacturers want to economize on material. However, this is an old version of the theory and may not be applicable today when 'dress-down' business clothing is more the norm.

S I D E B A R

'Dress-down days' a signifier of market tops

When I started work in the City in 1970, dark suits, white shirts, sober ties and black lace-up shoes were considered the minimum dress code for anyone who aspired to professional status.

The 1990s saw a proliferation of the phenomenon of 'dress-down' business casual attire, the so-called 'third wardrobe', much to the delight of up-market menswear retailers. This was when even sober partners in accountancy firms would don chinos and polo shirts in an attempt to mimic their racier brethren in the dot.com world.

I felt the phenomenon had reached its peak when I went to interview a senior investment banker. As is my wont when visiting the City, I put on a suit. The banker was dressed in jeans and an old sweater. In the 1980s, the reverse might have been the case. I still find it hard to take seriously the supposed professionals who feel their professional status is not compromised by casual attire.

The real point is that the vogue for dress-down clothing itself is a bull market indicator. If the labour market is tight, employees can dress casually with impunity. When markets are headed down and jobs are scarcer, employers can insist their employees revert to more normal business attire and stop making concessions. Employees themselves may even feel their career advancement may proceed faster if they look smart.

At the blue-blooded City broking firm of Cazenove, however, dressing down has never been the order of the day. Rumour has it that employees not wearing black lace-up shoes are sent home to change them. Even donning a striped shirt will bring comments that the individual in question has come to work in his pyjamas.

The second caveat is that a cynic might suggest that fashion deliberately rings the changes simply to make money. Changing the prevailing styles sharply from one season to the next and one year to the next is simply a way of selling more clothes to the fashion conscious rather than a harbinger of recession or expansion and tumbling or rising stock markets.

Why is it important for you?

Why should hemlines matter and why should the index work? If pop psychology is any guide, you might think that short skirts indicate exhibitionism and extreme levels of optimism, while long skirts indicate subconscious vulnerability, fear for the future and depression.

One can speculate endlessly along these lines. There are other related theories, too. One is the Lauder Lipstick index. The founders of Estée Lauder devised an index that measured lipstick sales, which seemed to indicate that lipsticks were bought more frequently in a recession because buyers of these products sought the comfort of small, affordable luxuries.

The Cocktail Party theory

Definition

Originally identified by the now-retired former Fidelity fund manager Peter Lynch in *One Up on Wall Street*, the theory relates to the crowd-like behaviour of many private investors.

Lynch claims the market cycle can be identified on the basis of people's reactions at cocktail parties when they discover his occupation. In the early stages of a bull market, people ask him for stock tips. In the late stage of a bull market people give him their stock tips. During a bear market people change the subject. At the bottom of a bear market people snub him.

Alternative names

None.

How it's calculated

The theory is simply based on anecdotal evidence.

Recent changes

I have no pretensions to be placed in the same category as Peter Lynch, who had few if any peers as a picker of superb small companies. But I have my own experiences of the Cocktail Party theory. As a financial journalist who writes about the stock market I also get asked for advice and occasionally get requests from companies to introduce them to stockbrokers or other sources of finance.

In late 1999 I was getting, completely unsolicited, a regular stream of e-mailed business plans and other proposals for dot.com start-ups, with requests to help them find investors or provide them with introductions to brokers. Needless to say the flow of e-mails of this type dried up pretty quickly after March 2000.

More recently the concerns of most investors I have met have centred on the value of their house and when and whether or not I think interest rates are likely to rise. Few people seem actively to be soliciting stock market tips the way they were a few years ago, thus neatly bearing out Lynch's theory.

Interpretation and why it's important for you

What you make of this theory depends on your point of view. For someone like me, it's easy to find out what people are thinking. I'm on the receiving end of the comments and requests for tips and other information. It takes a fairly self-aware investor to be conscious that they are starting to get carried away by their own enthusiasm for the market or are getting unduly depressed.

You need, as an investor, to have a questioning approach to your attitudes. Ultimately stock market values revert to some sort of logical basis, a touch-stone that is generally based around historical parallels, the value of a stream of discounted dividends and cash, and the risk-adjusted rate of return offered by other investments.

> You need, as an investor, to have a questioning approach to your attitudes.

If you find yourself getting too enthusiastic about the market and that values have diverged from this logical basis, and especially if you find yourself giving stock market tips to market commentators at cocktail parties, it's time to sell.

The R-word index

Definition

The 'R-word' is of course 'Recession', with a capital R. Again devised by *The Economist*, this theory suggests that mention of the R-word in newspaper articles does actually often pinpoint the beginnings of a recession.

Alternative names

None.

How it's calculated

The Economist has devised two indices. One takes the number of mentions of the word recession each quarter in the *New York Times* and *Washington Post* to measure the likelihood of recession in America. The other takes mentions in *The Wall Street Journal* and the *Financial Times*, to measure the likelihood of global recession. *The Economist* claims that this index accurately predicted the beginning of the 1981 and 1990 recessions and also signalled the start of the recent downturn.

Recent changes

The indicator began turning up in mid-2000 and increased sharply again in the third quarter of 2001 following the 11 September terrorist attacks. As of the third quarter of 2001, the rate of 'R-word' mentions was running at close to 1000 per quarter, still well under half the 1991 peak, suggesting that the downturn, at the time of writing, might have some way to run.

Interpretation and why it's important for you

The indicator tells you nothing particular about the stock market but it's a reasonably good signaller of the onset of recession. You can use it as a confirmation of the trends that might already have been suggested by other more conventional leading indicators (see Chapter 9).

The problem with accuracy of the R-word index in the context of the present setback could be, however, that we are facing more than recession and other words may be used as surrogates. In the aftermath of the biggest stock market bubble for 70 years there is talk of depression and deflation, two 'D-words' that might also be used as the basis of indicators themselves.

The odd-lot theory

Definition

The odd-lot theory starts from the presumption that the small-scale private investor is always wrong. Small investor activity in the US at least is measured by odd-lot trading. Odd lots are share parcels of less than 100 shares. Trading in 100 shares or multiples of it is regarded as a 'round lot'. By measuring the number of odd-lot trades and the respective volume of purchases and sales made in odd lots, market professionals can gauge what odd-lot investors are doing, and then do the opposite themselves.

Alternative names

Some books refer to the 'odd-lot ratio' and 'balance of odd-lot volume', another way of expressing the same information. Some US share-price-charting packages have the capability of calculating and graphing odd-lot activity.

How it's calculated

There are various methods of calculation. Typically odd-lot sales volume or value is deducted from or divided into odd-lot purchase volume or value to get the indicator, which may then be smoothed by use of a moving average to avoid 'spikiness' in the indicator.

Recent changes

Data on odd-lot trading in the US market is available from *The Wall Street Journal* and *The Wall Street Journal Europe*. In late June 2002 odd-lot purchases and sales by volume were running at 5:4 in favour of sales as recorded by floor-based market makers on the New York Stock Exchange. For all NYSE member firms, the figures showed sales and purchases more or less level. According to the conventional interpretation of the theory, this would be construed as marginally bullish. However, see general comments on interpretation below.

Interpretation

In his book *The Money Game* (Vintage Books, 1976), Adam Smith – a pen name, needless to say – describes the travails of Odd-lot Robert. Robert is a hapless private investor who starts investing with a bequest of $9000 and, at the time Smith encounters him, has run this down to $2100 through a series of bad investment decisions.

Most professional investors and market commentators, myself included, have met people like this. It seems to be true in some senses, but the odd-lot theory has a drawback.

It is that in general private investors have become more educated and more attuned to evaluating stocks and bonds in recent years. The result is that many of them behave more rationally than the theory might lead you to suppose. I suspect, too, that this may be the case even more in the future. Many typical odd-lot investors will have been taught searing lessons by the market collapse of early 2000 and will evaluate investments more cautiously and conservatively, and more thoroughly.

Market professionals themselves now generally regard the odd-lot theory as discredited. Rather like the put–call ratio, it may be fair to treat it at face value when it is showing values within normal bounds, and only use it as a contrary indicator when the readings are extreme, indicating an excessive level of speculation by small private investors.

My own signal for the top of the market was when a friend announced that his son, who had no previous stock market experience, was proposing to sell his house and use the proceeds to set himself up as an 'armchair investor', as though the business of trading was that simple. Fortunately for him the market crashed before he could put the plan into effect.

Many famous investors of the past have paid sharp attention to a combination of the odd-lot theory and the Cocktail Party phenomenon. The great Wall Street financier Bernard Baruch sold out of the market in the late 1920s when the liftboy at his office began giving him unsolicited stock tips.

So the odd-lot theory works to some degree, but often if you keep your eyes and ears open and your mouth shut, you may not need to calculate the ratio with any degree of precision. The evidence of over or undervaluation will be clear from the attitudes of those around you.

The put–call ratio

Definition

The put–call ratio uses data from the options market to make predictions about the level of the underlying market for shares as a whole. The term refers to the two different types of option that investors can buy, put options and call options.

A call option gives the holder of the option the right, but not the obligation, to buy a specified quantity of shares at a fixed exercise price for a pre-set length of time, after which the option expires. A put option gives the holder the right, but not the obligation, to sell a specified quantity of shares at a fixed exercise price for a pre-set length of time, after which the option expires.

Investors use call options to speculate on a rise in a share price and put options to speculate on a fall in price. This is because an options price will magnify any percentage change in the movement in the underlying shares. Options are an investment in gearing.

A call option moves in the same direction as the underlying share price, a put option the opposite way. Put options are often used as insurance to protect an existing shareholding against a possible fall in its price.

Because put and call options are used in this way, and because they are traded in contracts of a standard size through an organized market, the ratio of the volume of put option contracts to call option contracts can tell you something about the underlying bullishness or bearishness of option traders as a whole.

Alternative names

None.

How it's calculated

The put–call ratio is simply the volume of put option contracts traded divided by the number of call option contracts traded on any given day. The result is usually graphed over time to provide some perspective.

Recent changes

Information on the number of put option contracts and call option contracts traded is provided in publications like the *Financial Times* and *The Wall Street Journal*. There are web-based services that provide graphs of put–call ratios, particularly in the US market, where options are widely traded and data on option trading is readily available.

In late January 2002 the put–call ratio leant slightly towards put buyers, while in the UK the volume favoured call options by a ratio of 5:4. Neither indicator is particularly conclusive.

Interpretation and why it's important for you

Interpreting put–call ratios can be something of an art. The obvious point is that the higher the ratio, the more bearish sentiment is becoming. The more puts are being taken out, the more worried investors are about the stock or stock index and therefore are seeking to speculate on a fall or insure against it.

However, it isn't quite as simple as that. For one thing there are several different ways of measuring the put–call ratio. One way is to calculate the ratio for individual stocks, to find the degree of bullishness or bearishness at any given point in time. Many traders, however, confine their study of the put–call ratio to the option on a widely traded stock market index such as the S&P 500. This gives a broad view of market sentiment.

The second cause for care in interpreting the put-call ratio is that it is sometimes used as a contrary indicator. Particular extremes in put–call activity, a sharp upward spike in the index, indicating a climate of fear in the stock market, may in fact be a signal that it's right to buy, at least on a short–term basis. By the same token, if optimism is such that the put–call ratio is hitting new lows (more calls being bought than puts), then the chances are, as this gets to the extreme stage, the market is riding for a fall.

The big question is, when does normal bearishness or bullishness turn into panic selling or buying, and change into a sign that astute investors should do the opposite to the crowd? There is no precise way of discovering this and it is perhaps best to look for other signals to confirm the prevailing mood.

If the put–call ratio is hitting new lows, hemlines are dropping, and financial journalists and fund managers are being besieged at cocktails parties with punters suggesting their own tips, history might suggest the put–call ratio is telling you to sell.

There are other, more objective ways, of confirming this, which are dealt with in the next two sections.

The stock market capitalization to GDP ratio

Definition

This ratio divides GDP into the aggregate market value of the broadest possible stock market index and expresses the result as a percentage. The ratio has particular value when graphed over a lengthy period of time and is particularly good at spotting the development of stock market bubbles, although it is often only some time later that investors pay attention to what the index has been telling them.

Alternative names

None.

How it's calculated

See 'definition' above.

Recent changes

Table 10.2 shows the ratio of stock market value to GDP for some of the world's leading stock markets.

Interpretation and why it's important for you

The idea behind this calculation is to attempt to relate the value of the stock market to the value of the goods and services produced by the companies within it. There are a number of imperfections in the ratio, although over time it has shown a capacity to identify particularly extreme cases of stock market over-exuberance or depression.

The ratio is not particularly good for making judgements about the relative value of stock markets internationally. In other words, don't use the ratio to argue that the US stock market is undervalued because its ratio of stock market value to GDP is lower than Germany's.

The problems with interpreting the ratio arise essentially from the drawbacks outlined earlier when we looked at GDP itself, namely that GDP often does not show the whole picture – for various reasons.

The fact is that GDP has some limitations when it comes to measuring the true scale of economic activity within a country. GDP does not include any element of unpaid work or the scale of the so-called 'black economy' – transactions and payments for work done made in cash to avoid a tax liability or for other reasons. In some economies, as we noted earlier, this can represent a sizeable slug of economic activity and will quite possibly make the ratio of stock market value to GDP higher than it would otherwise be.

A further very important point is that the ratio can only measure the stock market value of those companies listed in a broad market index. It will not include the thousands of companies that fall outside the index. The index might typically cover the top listed 500 companies, for example, and so will take into account neither smaller listed companies nor indeed the value of unlisted private companies that contribute to the generation of GDP, nor any publicly owned corporations that do the same.

This means that countries with a large public sector in the form of nationalized industries (railways or perhaps electrical utilities and power generation) or which have a disproportionately large number of private companies relative to publicly listed ones will not have their value recorded in the numerator of the ratio, while their output will be in the denominator. This will tend to understate the ratio.

Table 10.2 Statistics on stock market valuations relative to normal GDP

Country	Approximate Value of stock market $bn	Approx GDP ($bn)	Ratio
USA	9860	7903	1.25
UK	2047	1264	1.62
France	775	1465	0.52
Germany	567	2180	0.26

Source: Author

There are big differences internationally in these items, another reason for simply looking at the ratio over time for a single country or stock market and not trying to make any comparisons between countries.

In the case of the non-inclusion of smaller listed companies, this objection can be largely dismissed. The top 500 companies will typically account for a percentage of the value of all listed companies that is in the high 90s and therefore the ratio will not be particularly affected by their omission.

Another reason for viewing the ratio with some circumspection is that stock markets are driven ultimately by corporate profitability and particularly by cash flow and dividends, and by factors that are incidental to GDP, such as interest rates. Small increases or decreases in GDP can produce much larger gains or expectation of gains in company profits, and hence drive stock markets.

Having said all that, it is only common sense that provided the GDP generated by listed companies remains a fairly constant proportion of the total, this should bear some relationship to the value of the stock market in the country concerned. Often the value fluctuates wildly. In the US, for example, the ratio of the capitalization of the Standard & Poors 500 (S&P 500, a broad market index) to nominal GDP in the US is currently 102%. In the period since the 1920s the ratio has typically peaked at around 90% of GDP. In subsequent recession it has troughed at a value of roughly 33% of GDP. The long-term average is around 50–60%.

At the height of the market mania in 1999 the ratio was standing at close to 160%, about three times the long-term average and slightly more than double the ratios seen at previous market peaks, including the major bull market tops in 1929 and 1972.

The ratio is clearly a sobering one for any would-be investor in the US stock market at current levels, since even to reach the average of the last 80 years, the index would have to fall 50% from its current level.

Tobin's Q ratio

Definition

The idea of the Q ratio (often known as Tobin's Q) was first mooted by economist James Tobin in 1969. In broad terms its main assumption is that listed companies should be valued at their underlying net worth, that is, the value of their accounting net asset value.

Alternative names

Net asset value is sometimes called 'book' value, especially where US markets are concerned. Some purists use the replacement cost of net assets as the denominator for the Q ratio, but this is somewhat harder to find with any degree of accuracy. Similarly, some calculations exclude the value of land from the asset calculation.

How it's calculated

Index providers and some statistical services provide the data giving the market capitalization of index constituents and their aggregate net asset value. Dividing aggregate market capitalization by aggregate net asset (or book) value allows the derivation of the Q ratio.

> Net asset value is sometimes called 'book' value, especially where US markets are concerned.

Recent changes

The best source for data about 'Q' is at Smithers & Co's website at **www.smithers.co.uk**. This has a downloadable spreadsheet giving values for Q and the underlying data going back to the early years of the century. Andrew Smithers was the co-author of *Valuing Wall Street*, which is the definitive work on Q and how it has varied over the years.

As of October 2001, the data for Q showed the ratio standing at around 1.58, significantly below the peak level reached when the market was at its most manic, but still considerably above the long-term average, which Smithers calculates as being 0.68.

Interpretation and why it's important for you

Q is a basic measure of whether stock markets are in touch with reality. Very often they aren't. Smithers describes it as being like a piece of elastic that will pull any deviation from the long-term average back to it in the fullness of time, as indeed seems to be happening at present. This is a well-established statistical principle known as reversion to the mean (where 'mean' signifies the average).

Critics of the ratio point to the fact that in the new economy companies are much less dependent on physical assets to make money and much more dependent on human capital and intellectual capital. Consequently the old relationship between book assets and stock market value may not hold true.

It is, however, precisely this argument that was used to justify the outlandish valuations on technology companies in the final stages of the last bull market. It is also incorrect.

Unless intellectual capital is genuinely created, all other forms of intangible asset usually arise as a result of acquisitions, in other words they are paid for out of a company's retained profits and hence are fully reflected in net asset value, which is itself merely the cumulative total of retained profits over the course of the company's life.

Equally, to the extent that intangible assets have been acquired, this means they have been acquired from their old owner at more than their book cost.

The net effect of the transaction is to transfer the difference in book value – whether positive or negative – from the new owner to the old owner. In total for the economy as a whole, the effect is neutral (a debit for the buyer is a credit for the seller and vice versa) and the same is therefore likely to be true for the stock market as a whole. No new value has been created; the old value has simply been allocated in a different way.

Even the creation of intellectual capital by one company may well be to the detriment of the value of the intellectual capital and intangible assets of another. The invention of the word processor decimated typewriter sales, personal computer sales hit mainframe computer sales, the launch of one type of software will affect sales of a competitor and so on.

All of these factors mean it is important to remember that Q is more valid for the market as a whole than for individual companies and often more valuable than some market commentators give it credit for.

The Q ratio is only one of a series of tools one can employ to check whether or not the market's valuation is realistic. But it is a useful one.

IN BRIEF

- Indicators that monitor investor behaviour and patterns of activity in the markets over a long period are widely followed. Many use everyday metaphors.

- The Big Mac index measures the real purchasing power of currencies. Some investors claim the length of women's skirts can predict the course of the stock market.

- The behaviour of small investors at market peaks and troughs is often a contrary indicator of what will happen next. Several indicators measure this.

- Increasingly frequent mentions of recession in newspaper articles often mean one is about to happen.

- Ratios that relate the aggregate value of a stock market's listed companies to real-world measures such as GDP or aggregate net asset value can highlight long-term over or undervaluation of the stock market.

Appendix 1 Glossary

Advance release calendar A list giving the dates when particular key economic indicators will be announced by an official statistics organization.

Annualize To convert monthly or quarterly growth rates into their annual equivalent.

Arithmetic mean An average calculated by adding together a series of figures and dividing by the number of them.

Assembly rate A method of calculating car manufacturing statistics in the US.

At factor cost A method of calculating gross domestic product by adding together the cost of its various inputs.

Average earnings Statistics of earnings that include bonuses and overtime payments as well as normal wages.

Bank base rate The rate of interest charged by banks to their most creditworthy customers.

Black economy Unrecorded cash transactions, and the activity behind them.

Blue-chip companies High-quality financially sound businesses.

Broad money A measure of money supply that includes not just notes and coins but also bank credit and securities transactions of various types.

Business capital structure The way in which a company is financed, usually through a mixture of equity and debt.

Business spending The corporate counterpart to consumer spending. Business spending is usually on capital equipment and other tangible and intangible assets.

Cable Jargon for the sterling/dollar exchange rate.

Call option The right, but not the obligation, to buy at a fixed price for a period of time into the future.

Capacity utilization A measure of the degree to which there is unused production capacity in the economy.

Capital account The part of foreign trade statistics that measures flows of money rather than goods and services.

Capital formation Spending by businesses on capital equipment.

Claimant count Measure of the unemployed that uses only those workers claiming unemployment benefit.

Collateralized loans Borrowing, usually in securities transactions, that is secured against high-quality assets such as government bonds.

Commercial paper Short-term tradeable debt issued by companies to finance working capital.

Composite leading indicator A measure combining several different statistics that tend to move ahead of the economy.

Consensus forecast The 'general view' of market commentators.

Constant prices Statistics calculated so as to exclude the effect of price changes.

Consumer expenditure What individuals spend on goods and services for their personal use.

Contrary opinion theory Stock market theory that suggests that whatever the crowd does is wrong.

Correlation The degree to which two or more variables appear to move in tandem.

Cross rate A rate of exchange between two specific currencies.

Currency future A contract to buy or sell a specific amount of currency in the future at a price agreed at the time the deal is struck.

Current account The balance of trade in goods and services (as opposed to the capital account, which measures the balance of flows of money and investment).

Deficit spending The deliberate running of a budget deficit by a government, in order to apply some stimulus to the domestic economy.

Deflating Adjusting statistics to exclude the impact of price inflation.

Deflation A significant period of falling rather than rising prices. The opposite of inflation.

Deflator Multiplier used to adjust statistics for changes in price levels over time.

Disaggregate A statistical term meaning to separate a statistical series into its component parts.

Discount rate A short-term interest rate. Originally the rate at which short-term bills were discounted by the central bank for cash.

Dollar GDP The accepted international measure of the size of an economy – its GDP expressed in terms of US dollars.

Durable goods In consumer spending statistics, items that are bought and kept for a number of years (cars, domestic appliances and the like).

Econometric models Computer models which attempt to measure and forecast the economy in a mathematically precise way.

Economic growth Normally the change in GDP on an annual or quarter-by-quarter basis.

Establishment survey A survey of businesses to determine employment data.

Fed funds rate A short-term interest rate in the US.

Federal Reserve The US central bank.

'Flash' numbers Statistics released as soon as possible after compilation, often subsequently revised.

Forward rates Exchange rates quoted for future delivery. These differ from futures contracts.

Free cash flow Cash generated by companies after paying tax, interest and sufficient in capital spending to maintain their assets.

Frictional unemployment 'Normal' unemployment that is the result of the ebbs and flows in the economy.

GDP deflator The multiplier used to get from nominal to 'real' GDP, that is excluding inflation.

Geometric mean An average constructed by multiplying together 'n' numbers and then taking the 'n'th root of the product.

Government consumption Spending by the government on items purchased for the public sector. This excludes social security and unemployment benefits.

Gross domestic fixed capital formation Another name for the aggregate of capital spending by corporations.

Headline rate A rate of growth or some other measure that is the most prominently presented or most often commented upon.

Hemline index A not entirely serious theory that relates stock market movements to the rise and fall of ladies' hemlines.

Hot money Speculative flows of capital, frequently disrupting currency markets.

Hyperinflation A period of extremely rapid inflation.

ILO unemployment A particular definition of unemployment set by the ILO for the purposes of making international comparisons.

Index numbers A way of presenting statistics using a single year as a base level of 100, with subsequent years' raw statistics divided by that of the base year to arrive at a number that is easily comparable.

Index tracker funds Mutual funds/unit trusts that attempt to mimic exactly the movement of a specific stock market index.

Industrial production The output of physical goods by a range of industries in a country. Distinct from manufacturing output as it also includes mining and other extractive industries and power generation.

Input prices The prices of raw materials, such as fuel, used by industry.

Intellectual capital Assets such as copyrights, patents, designs, software licences, and trade marks.

Interest rate futures Contracts to buy or sell money for delivery at a specific time in the future at today's rate of interest.

Intermediate goods Manufactured components used by industrial companies.

Invisible exports Services such as shipping and insurance that are sold to foreign buyers.

Key indicators A small set of statistics that encapsulates the overall performance of an economy – GDP growth, unemployment, the trade balance, inflation and so on.

Lagging and coincident indicators Sets of statistics that lag behind (move after) or coincide with changes in economic conditions in a country.

Leads and lags The distorting of payments statistics by the fact that orders for goods and services and payment for them may be speeded up or slowed down for unconnected reasons.

LIBOR London Inter Bank Offered Rate, a key international benchmark for interest rates.

Long bond The US 30-year Treasury bond.

Macro-economic analysis Analysis of broad economic trends.

Manufacturing output The value of production of manufactured goods. This excludes extractive industries and utilities.

Market sentiment The general good or bad humour of buyers and sellers in the stock market as a whole.

Misery index An index that measures the combined effect of inflation and unemployment.

Monetary aggregates A synonym for the different measures of money supply.

Monetary Policy Committee A committee convened by the Bank of England for the purpose of setting interest rates.

Money supply The overall stock of money in an economy, including notes, coins and various types of bank credit.

Moving average An average that combines a successively changing series of variables. Moving averages eliminate short-term volatility and allow an underlying trend to be better discerned.

Narrow money A strict definition of money supply that primarily includes just notes and coins.

Non-accelerating inflation rate of unemployment (NAIRU) The lowest level of unemployment in an economy that can be sustained without any further reductions leading to upward pressure on wages and prices.

Non-durable goods Consumer goods that are consumed quickly – food, drink, tobacco and so on.

Open market operations Operations a central bank conducts in the money markets in order to control the rate of growth of money supply, normally by buying and selling government securities.

Payroll A US term for numbers employed in a business. US payroll numbers are measures of numbers employed.

Personal expenditure Another term for consumer spending.

Personal savings Income that is not spent by individuals.

Plant and machinery Factories, buildings, machines, vehicles and the like that are owned by businesses.

Productivity Output per man hour or per unit of wage cost.

Public spending The broadest definition of spending by government and government-owned corporations. In contrast to government consumption, this figure will normally include spending on social security and other benefits.

Purchasing power parity A way of measuring exchange rates by reference to what individuals within a country can buy with a unit of their currency. Countries where the cost of living is low may have PPP rate of exchange that exceeds the nominal rate of exchange.

Put option The right, but not the obligation, to sell at a predetermined price for a specified length of time in the future.

Put–call ratio The ratio of the number of put option contracts traded in a stock market divided by the volume of call options. Sometimes used as a contrary indicator of market direction.

Real Adjusted for inflation. The opposite of nominal.

Regression analysis Statistical analysis that attempts to calculate a 'line of best fit' through a series of observations such as, for example, daily share prices.

Repo rate A key market rate of interest. The rate implied by the terms of repurchase (repo) agreements. Repos are collateralized loans used by traders for finance and gearing purposes.

Reserve currencies Major currencies that are universally accepted in international transactions. These days, the dollar and the Euro.

Residual Data that is arrived at by calculating what remains after other constituents have been deducted.

Retail banking Banking services for the private individual.

Reversion to the mean The tendency of many series of variables to trend back towards their average value.

R-word Recession.

Sample A carefully selected subgroup whose characteristics are measured in order to infer the characteristics of the larger group as a whole.

Saving ratio The percentage of household income represented by savings.

Schengen Group Group of EU countries that have effectively abolished border controls.

Seasonal adjustments Adjustments that attempt to isolate and remove the recurring effects on statistics of changes in demand due to the different times of year.

Soft commodities Commodities such as wheat, coffee, cocoa and the like.

Spending basket A representative selection of goods whose prices are measured to calculate changes in retail prices as a whole.

Spot rate The current rate of exchange.

Standard deviation A measure of the degree to which a group of variables is dispersed from the average.

Stratified random sample A sample chosen randomly, but reflecting the relative importance of different subgroups within the whole.

Structural unemployment Unemployment that results from the long-term rise and fall of major industries.

Terms of trade The relationship between the international price of a country's exports and the cost of its imports.

Tobin tax A transaction tax, originally proposed by economist James Tobin, to eliminate large-scale speculation in foreign currencies.

Tobin's Q The ratio of a stock market's total value to the book value of the companies listed on it.

Total employment costs The total costs borne by businesses as a result of employing workers, including not only wages and salaries but also pension entitlements and the like.

Transfer payments Payments that do not represent the result of any economic activity or production. Social security payments are transfers from taxpayers to those on benefit.

Variance The aggregate of squared deviations from a mean or average.

Visible trade International trade in goods, rather than 'invisibles'.

Volatility The amplitude of the swings in a variable around its central trend. In stock market terms, volatility is often equated to risk.

Wealth effect The impact of changes in the stock market on consumer confidence and therefore on consumption and economic activity.

Weighting Adjusting the relative importance of one variable versus another dependent on its size or scale. Changes in the US economy would carry more weight in a statistical measure than a similar change in the British economy, which is appreciably smaller.

Yield curve A graph plotting the yields on government bonds of successively longer maturity.

Appendix 2 Abbreviations

BEA	Bureau of Economic Affairs
CBI	Confederation of British Industry
CD	certificate of deposit
CIPS	Chartered Institute of Purchasing and Supply
CPI	consumer price index
CPI-U	consumer price index – Urban
DAX	Deutsch Aktien IndeX (the German benchmark stock market index)
ECB	European Central Bank
EIU	Economist Intelligence Unit
ERM	Exchange Rate Mechanism
EU	European Union
EURIBOR	Euro Inter Bank Offered Rate
G7	Group of Seven (leading industrial countries)
GDP	gross domestic product
GNP	gross national product
GVA	gross value added
HICP	Harmonized Index of Consumer Prices
HIPC	highly indebted poor countries
ILO	International Labour Organization
IMF	International Monetary Fund
ISM	Institute for Supply Management
ITEM	Independent Treasury Economic Model (a forecasters' club)
LIBOR	London Inter Bank Offered Rate
LIFFE	London International Financial Futures and Options Exchange
M0–M5	abbreviations for different measures of money stock
NAIRU	Non-accelerating inflation rate of unemployment
NAMP	National Association of Purchasing Managers
NIESR	National Institute of Economic and Social Research
NNI	net national income
OECD	Organization for Economic Cooperation and Development
ONS	Office for National Statistics
OPEC	Organization of Petroleum Exporting Countries
PDI	personal disposal index
PPI	producer price indices
PPP	purchasing power parity
PSBR	public sector borrowing requirement
RPI	retail price index
RPIX	retail price index (exchange mortgage interest payments)
S&P	Standard & Poors
SMMT	Society of Motor Manufacturers and Traders
SONIA	Sterling Over Night Index Average

Appendix 3 Further reading

The following is a selection of books that readers may find helpful. The dates of publication refer to the editions in my possession. In some instances a more up-to-date edition may have been issued.

Title	Author(s)	Publisher
Statistics without Tears	Derek Rowntree	Penguin 1981
Pocket World in Figures	*The Economist*	Profile 2000
How to Lie with Statistics	Darrell Huff	Penguin 1991
Guide to Economic Indicators	*The Economist*	Profile 2000
The Fortune Sellers	William Sherden	Wiley 1998
Introducing Statistics	Keith Yeomans	Penguin 1968
Applied Statistics	Keith Yeomans	Penguin 1968
Economics	Paul Samuelson	McGraw Hill 1964
Reflections on Monetarism	Tim Congdon	Edward Elgar 1992
Key Economic Indicators	Mark Rogers	McGraw Hill 1998
Valuing Wall Street	Smithers/Wright	McGraw Hill 2000
International Economics	Charles Kindleberger	Irwin 1968
The General Theory of Employment, Interest and Money	JM Keynes	Macmillan 1967

Index